a passion for *tapas*

a passion for *tapas*

Love Food ™ is an imprint of Parragon Books Ltd

Parragon
Queen Street House
4 Queen Street
Bath BA1 1HE, UK

Copyright © Parragon Books Ltd 2007

Love Food ™ and the accompanying heart device is a trademark of Parragon Books Ltd

ISBN 978-1-4054-9447-2

Internal design by Jane Bozzard-Hill
Cover design by Mark Cavanagh
Photography by Günter Beer and Laurie Evans
Home economy by Stevan Paul and Carol Tennant
Introduction by Beverly LeBlanc

Printed in China

Notes for the reader
This book uses imperial, metric, and US cup measurements. Follow the same units of
measurement throughout; do not mix imperial and metric. All spoon measurements are
level, unless otherwise stated: teaspoons are assumed to be 5 ml, and tablespoons are
assumed to be 15 ml. Unless otherwise stated, milk is assumed to be whole, eggs and
individual fruits such as bananas are medium, and pepper is freshly ground black pepper.

Recipes using raw or very lightly cooked eggs should be avoided by infants, the elderly,
pregnant women, convalescents, and anyone suffering from an illness. Pregnant and
breast-feeding women are advised to avoid eating peanuts and peanut products.

contents

Introduction   6

Vegetables, Nuts & Olives   12

Meat & Poultry   54

Fish & Seafood   96

Eggs & Cheese   138

Bread   180

Index   222

Introduction

Welcome to the world of Spanish tapas culture. Tapas are small, bite-sized morsels of tasty food, like finger food, that are uniquely Spanish. Tapas are served in Spanish bars and cafes throughout the day, and the preparation, eating, and enjoyment of tapas are essential parts of everyday Spanish life. It can be tempting to describe tapas as the Spanish version of French hors d'oeuvres or Mediterranean meze, but they are very different. Unlike meze, for example, tapas are never intended to replace a proper meal, nor do they form the first course of a meal, such as is the role of hors d'oeuvres.

"Tapas are a national obsession of endless variety"

The Spanish rarely drink alcohol without eating, so wherever you travel in this vast country you will find people standing at bars nibbling bite-sized meat-, poultry-, vegetable-, and seafood-based tapas with their drinks, be it late morning, lunchtime, mid-afternoon, or in the evening before going home for a late supper. Older Spaniards fondly remember when simple tapas—a bowl of almonds or olives, slices of bread drizzled with olive oil, or chunks of chorizo—were always served free with any drink. That tradition, unfortunately, hasn't stood the test of time, but there hasn't been any decline in the popularity of tapas themselves.

The Spanish word *tapa* means "lid," and the nation's obsession with these flavorsome tidbits began hundreds of years ago when Andalusian innkeepers used slices of bread to keep dust and bugs out of the glasses of wine and sherry provided for passing horsemen. Eventually slices of ham and cheese were added to the bread, and tapas as we know them today were born, evolving from the arid landscape of southern Spain into a national obsession of endless variety. In fact, sampling a selection of tapas is a good overall introduction to the exciting flavors of Spanish cuisine.

Tapas bars are called tascas, and they are very egalitarian establishments, where wine barons, bankers, and industrialists rub shoulders with farm workers, students, parents with children, and even tourists. Unlike American bars or English pubs, however, the raison d'être of tapas bars puts conversations and rendez-vous ahead of simply drinking. Tapas bars always have a convivial atmosphere with background buzz of friends and neighbors meeting, greeting, and chatting.

If the bar is in a tourist area you might be given a menu, often with photographs to overcome language problems, but otherwise don't expect one. Some tapas bars list the daily offerings on a chalkboard, or you make your selection from the prepared tapas displayed in glass cabinets on the bar. In most of Spain the bartender or a waiter or waitress will serve you, but in the Basque Country it is traditional for customers to help themselves.

As universal as the word "tapas" is, not all tapas are the same, as there are several categories. *Cosas de picar*, which literally means "little things to nibble" are the simplest, such as a bowl of salted almonds, olives, or cubes of cheese. These are, of course, the easiest tapas for you to serve with drinks before dinner. *Pinchos*, however, can be a bit more substantial and are easily recognized because they are speared with flat wooden toothpicks called *banderillas*, which resemble the darts used in bullfighting. *Cazuelas*, a type of tapas with a sauce and often hot, are so called because they are usually served in the small, brown glazed earthenware dishes also called *cazuelas*. Sizzling Chile Shrimp (see page 121), Chicken Livers in Sherry Sauce (see page 92), and Fava Beans with Ham (see page 37) are examples of popular *cazuelas*. These are ideal to serve to guests with drinks before dinner when you don't want to serve a first course at the table. *Montaditos* is the word to describe slices of French bread generously topped with mayonnaise-based salads, such as potato salad, tuna salad (see page 200), or salt cod (see page 190), which are served throughout the country. Part of the popularity of this type of tapas has to be that they are inexpensive and easy to prepare. *Bocadillos*, on the other hand, are small, more conventional sandwiches with a simple filling between two slices of bread. Roast loin of pork, cured ham, spicy sausage, cheese, and thin omelets are typical fillings. *Rebozadas* are the fried fritters Spaniards are so fond of—try Zucchini Fritters with a Dipping Sauce (see page 25).

"Tapas culture is most obvious in larger cities"

By convention tapas aren't intended to be a meal, but when you see a tapas described as a *racione*, it will be more filling than most and could be just what you are looking for at lunchtime to accompany a glass of chilled *vino blanco*.

As you look through the recipes in this book, you'll see that preparing tapas offers plenty of scope for experimentation and that they can be assembled from the simplest pantry ingredients (see page 11). Tapas are particularly suited to entertaining, because they can be made well in advance, so you can enjoy the gathering as much as your guests.

Tapas Culture

You'll find tapas in every small village or town, but the height of tapas culture is most obvious in larger cities, where the nightly pilgrimage from tapas bar to tapas bar is called *tapeo*. It's a slow, relaxed procession as friends congregate at one bar to catch up on the day's news over a small glass of *fino* sherry, wine, or a chilled draft beer with, perhaps, a crisp, deep-fried salt-cod fritter or a slice of tortilla, before casually meandering on to the next bar for more conversation, another drink, and perhaps a few cubes of sizzling chorizo or fried, batter-coated squid rings. It's all part of the ebb and flow of the evening that a bar can be packed like a sardine can and then be virtually empty 30 minutes later, before filling up again.

Of course, regional specialties change as you travel across the country, but some tapas you will find everywhere include Spanish Tortilla, a thick egg and potato omelet; crisp, deep-fried zucchini; wafer-thin slices of Serrano ham; finely diced potato salad to spread on slices of bread; and bowls of salted, toasted almonds.

Seville and the other Andalucian cities of Granada, Cadiz, and Cordoba have a lively tapas tradition, but the *tapeo* is also part of living and working in Madrid and San Sebastian. The small, winding streets behind Madrid's Plaza Mayor are where the locals gather for their nightly tapas.

In the northern Basque Country all food, be it simple marinated anchovy fillets on bread or a three-course meal in a Michelin-starred restaurant, is taken seriously, very seriously indeed. Not surprisingly, tapas in the stylish city of San Sebastian are unlike anywhere else. For a start, the nightly bar crawl is *txikiteo* and tapas are called *pintxos*, the Basque word for *pinchos*, because they are almost always speared with a toothpick. Even a slice of tortilla is served on bread with a toothpick securing the two ingredients together.

Bars in the oldest part of San Sebastian compete to see which can offer the most tempting selection. It's not unusual to see thirty or more platters of tapas arranged on the bar with small wooden stands, like cake stands, used to create extra space for a second layer of platters.

When you order your drink at the bar, just ask for a plate and make your selection from all the appetizing-looking morsels. For a taste of Basque cuisine, try Anchovy Rolls (see page 199), Salt Cod on Garlic Toasts (see page 190), Basque Scrambled Eggs (see page 160), and Deep-Fried Green Chiles (see page 20). When you are ready to move on to the next bar, the barman will simply count the number of toothpicks on your plate to calculate your bill. If you want to look like a local, throw your paper napkins onto the floor.

Interestingly, Barcelona, Spain's second largest city and capital of Catalunya, doesn't have a long history of tapas culture. It is only in recent years, as improved transportation and communications have blurred regional distinctions throughout the country, not just in Catalunya, that large tapas bars have appeared. Look for the bars called *xampanyerias*. Once unique to Barcelona, these bars specialize in tapas and cava, the Spanish sparkling wine.

"Recreate the flavors of Spain's tapas bars at home"

One of the great joys of tapas is that they are easy to prepare and can be made using ingredients that are widely available—in fact, it is likely that you will have many of them in your pantry already. However, it is worth hunting out some of the more unusual items—these can be purchased from large supermarkets or gourmet food stores. The following ingredients will help you to recreate the flavors of Spain's tapas bars at home.

Almonds *(almendras)* A bowl of blanched almonds is one of the easiest tapas you can serve, but if you want to be more ambitious, try Salted Almonds (see page 14) or Tiny Meatballs in Almond Sauce (see page 64). For freshness, buy unblanched and blanch just before using—just drop the nuts in boiling water for a few minutes, then drain and refresh under cold water. Use your fingers to squeeze the nuts so they pop out of the skins.

Cheese *(queso)* Many of Spain's numerous cheeses feature in tapas selections. For a simple tapas, serve slices of Manchego, a sheep's milk cheese from La Mancha, or cubes of Cabrales, a rich bleu cheese, with drinks. Croquettes are a thrifty way to make use of the small pieces of leftover cheese.

Cured meats *(charcutería)* Spanish tapas cooks make great use of cured pork, lamb, and beef, and anyone visiting Spain for the first time will be dazzled by the quantity of packets in supermarkets, sliced and ready for putting on plates for serving. Serrano or Mountain ham *(jamón serrano)*, perhaps the best known, features at many tapas bars—it can be served in thin slices, as a sandwich filling, or on bread topped with vegetables. Plain cooked ham is *jamón cocida*, also used in tapas. The most highly regarded will be labeled as Iberico, and you'll recognize it by the hefty price. Other less well known, but equally popular, charcuterie include boneless pork loin *(lomo)* and Spain's ubiquitous pork sausage, the spicy chorizo, colored with paprika.

Garlic *(ajo)* An essential Spanish flavoring. Buy fresh and use within a month once the head has been broken into.

Legumes *(legumbres secas)* Spanish kitchen cupboards contain many jars and tins of legumes, including butter beans *(alubia de Perú)*, chickpeas *(garbanzos)*, and lentils *(lentejas)*, ready to use without having to go to the trouble of overnight soaking and boiling first. Chickpeas & Chorizo (see page 79) is a typical tapas, bursting with flavor and easy to prepare.

Olive oil *(aceite de oliva)* Spain is the world's largest olive oil producer, so it is a regular feature of Spanish cooking; butter is rarely used. Heat destroys the flavor of oil so save your best, and most expensive, extra virgin oil for uncooked dishes and cook with plain olive oil.

Paprika *(pimentón)* Made from ground, dried red peppers, paprika adds a mild or strong smoky flavor and vibrant red color to dishes. It's one of the essential flavors of chorizo and many Spanish dishes.

Pimientos del piquillo Take a tip from Spanish cooks and always keep a jar of these grilled and skinned bell peppers in your pantry. They come bottled in olive oil or brine, either whole or sliced, and take the work out of serving roasted bell peppers.

Saffron *(azafrán)* Good-quality Spanish saffron comes from La Mancha and is expensive. Saffron Shrimp with Lemon Mayonnaise (see page 122) is a good recipe to showcase the spice's unrivaled golden color and distinctive flavor. Enhance the flavor by lightly toasting before using. Store in a sealed container.

Canned fish There is a wide range of preserved fish available, including anchovies *(boquerones)*, sardines *(sardines)*, and tuna *(atún)*. Buy fish preserved in olive oil for the best flavor.

vegetables, nuts & olives

Tapas bars can be a culinary heaven for vegetable lovers in Spain, a land of serious meat eaters. This chapter contains a wealth of vegetable recipes, celebrating Spain's position as gardener to Europe. Roasted bell peppers and zucchini always add color and flavor to tapas menus.

Spanish cooks never run out of ideas for preparing potatoes, but Patatas Bravas, so called because of the hot chili sauce, are one of the country's favorite tapas. Try it and you'll understand why.

Finally, what could be more quintessentially Spanish than nibbling a bowl of Olives with Orange & Lemon while sipping a cold drink?

salted almonds

SERVES 6–8
as part of a tapas meal

8 oz/225 g whole almonds,
   in their skins or blanched
4 tbsp Spanish olive oil
coarse sea salt
1 tsp paprika or ground cumin
   (optional)

Preheat the oven to 350°F/180°C. Fresh almonds in their skins are superior in taste, but blanched almonds are much more convenient. If the almonds are not blanched, place them in a large bowl, cover with boiling water for 3–4 minutes, then drain and plunge them into cold water for 1 minute. Drain them well in a strainer, then slide off the skins between your fingers. Dry the almonds well on paper towels.

Place the olive oil in a roasting pan and swirl it around so that it covers the base. Add the almonds and toss them in the pan so that they are evenly coated in the oil, then spread them out in a single layer.

Roast the almonds in the preheated oven for 20 minutes, or until they are light golden brown, tossing several times during the cooking. Drain the almonds on paper towels, then transfer them to a bowl.

While the almonds are still warm, sprinkle with plenty of sea salt and paprika, if using, and toss together to coat. Serve the almonds warm or cold. The almonds are at their best when served freshly cooked so, if possible, cook them on the day that you plan to eat them. However, they can be stored in an airtight container for up to 3 days.

spicy cracked marinated olives

SERVES 8
as part of a tapas meal

2¹/₂ cups canned or jarred large
    green Spanish olives, drained
4 garlic cloves, peeled
2 tsp coriander seeds
1 small lemon
4 fresh thyme sprigs
4 feathery stalks of fennel
2 small fresh red chiles
    (optional)
pepper
Spanish extra virgin olive oil

If using unpitted olives, place them on a cutting board and, using a rolling pin, bash them lightly so that they crack slightly. Alternatively, use a sharp knife to cut a lengthwise slit in each olive as far as the pit. Using the flat side of a broad knife, lightly crush each garlic clove. Using a mortar and pestle, crack the coriander seeds. Cut the lemon, with its rind, into small chunks.

Place the olives, garlic, coriander seeds, lemon chunks, thyme sprigs, fennel, and chiles, if using, in a large bowl and toss together. Season to taste with pepper, but you should not need to add salt as canned or jarred olives are usually salty enough. Pack the ingredients tightly into a glass jar with a lid. Pour in enough olive oil to cover the olives, then seal the jar tightly.

Let the olives stand at room temperature for 24 hours, then marinate in the refrigerator for at least 1 week but preferably 2 weeks before serving. From time to time, gently give the jar a shake to re-mix the ingredients. Return the olives to room temperature and remove from the oil to serve. Provide wooden toothpicks for spearing the olives.

olives with orange & lemon

Dry-roast the fennel seeds and cumin seeds in a small, heavy-bottom skillet, shaking the skillet frequently, until they begin to pop and give off their aroma. Remove the skillet from the heat and let cool.

Place the olives, orange and lemon rind, shallots, cinnamon, and roasted seeds in a bowl.

Whisk the vinegar, olive oil, orange juice, mint, and parsley together in a bowl and pour over the olives. Toss well, then cover and let chill for 1–2 days before serving.

SERVES 4–6
as part of a tapas meal

2 tsp fennel seeds
2 tsp cumin seeds
1¼ cups green Spanish olives
1¼ cups black Spanish olives
2 tsp grated orange rind
2 tsp grated lemon rind
3 shallots, finely chopped
pinch of ground cinnamon
4 tbsp white wine vinegar
5 tbsp Spanish extra virgin
  olive oil
2 tbsp orange juice
1 tbsp chopped fresh mint
1 tbsp chopped fresh parsley

deep-fried green chiles

SERVES 4–6
as part of a tapas meal

Spanish olive oil, for frying
9 oz/250 g sweet or hot fresh
  chiles
sea salt

Heat 3 inches/7.5 cm of oil in a large, heavy-bottom pan until it reaches 350–375°F/180–190°C, or until a cube of bread turns brown in 30 seconds.

Rinse the chiles and pat them very dry with paper towels. Drop them in the hot oil for no longer than 20 seconds, or until they turn bright green and the skins blister.

Remove with a slotted spoon and drain well on crumpled paper towels. Sprinkle with sea salt and serve immediately.

sautéed garlic mushrooms

SERVES 6
as part of a tapas meal

1 lb/450 g button mushrooms
5 tbsp Spanish olive oil
2 garlic cloves, finely chopped
lemon juice
salt and pepper
4 tbsp chopped fresh parsley
lemon wedges, for garnish
crusty bread, for serving

Wipe or brush clean the mushrooms, then trim the stems. Cut any large mushrooms in half or into quarters. Heat the olive oil in a large, heavy-bottom skillet. Add the garlic and cook for 30 seconds–1 minute, or until lightly browned. Add the mushrooms and sauté over high heat, stirring frequently, until the mushrooms have absorbed all the oil in the skillet.

Reduce the heat to low. When the juices have come out of the mushrooms, increase the heat again and sauté for 4–5 minutes, stirring frequently, until the juices have almost evaporated. Add a squeeze of lemon juice and season to taste with salt and pepper. Stir in the parsley and cook for an additional 1 minute.

Transfer the sautéed mushrooms to a warmed serving dish, then garnish with lemon wedges and serve piping hot or warm. Accompany with crusty bread for mopping up the juices.

zucchini fritters with a dipping sauce

To make the pine nut sauce, place the pine nuts and garlic in a food processor and process to form a purée. With the motor still running, gradually add the olive oil, lemon juice, and water to form a smooth sauce. Stir in the parsley and season to taste with salt and pepper. Transfer to a serving bowl and reserve until needed.

To prepare the zucchini, cut them on the diagonal into thin slices about 1/4 inch/5 mm thick. Place the flour and paprika in a plastic bag and mix together. Beat the egg and milk together in a large bowl.

Add the zucchini slices to the flour mixture and toss well together until coated. Shake off the excess flour. Heat the corn oil in a large, heavy-bottom skillet to a depth of about 1/2 inch/1 cm. Dip the zucchini slices, one at a time, into the egg mixture, then slip them into the hot oil. Cook the zucchini slices in batches in a single layer so that they do not overcrowd the skillet, for 2 minutes, or until they are crisp and golden brown.

Using a slotted spoon, remove the zucchini fritters from the skillet and drain on paper towels. Continue until all the zucchini slices have been fried.

Serve the zucchini fritters piping hot, lightly sprinkled with sea salt, and accompanied by the pine nut sauce for dipping.

**SERVES 6–8
as part of a tapas meal**

1 lb/450 g baby zucchini
3 tbsp all-purpose flour
1 tsp paprika
1 large egg
2 tbsp milk
corn oil, for pan-frying
coarse sea salt

for the pine nut sauce
2/3 cup pine nuts
1 garlic clove, peeled
3 tbsp Spanish extra virgin
   olive oil
1 tbsp lemon juice
3 tbsp water
1 tbsp chopped fresh flat-leaf
   parsley
salt and pepper

deep-fried artichoke hearts

SERVES 4–6
as part of a tapas meal

½ cup self-rising flour
¼ tsp salt
¼ tsp hot or sweet smoked
   Spanish paprika
1 garlic clove, crushed
5 tbsp water
1 tbsp olive oil
juice of ½ lemon
12 small globe artichokes
sunflower or Spanish olive oil,
   for deep-frying
aïoli (see page 50), for serving

To make the batter, put the flour, salt, paprika, and garlic in a large bowl and make a well in the center. Gradually pour the water and olive oil into the well and mix in the flour mixture from the side, beating constantly, until all the flour is incorporated and a smooth batter forms. Let rest while preparing the artichokes.

Fill a bowl with cold water and add the lemon juice. Cut off the stalks of the artichokes. With your hands, break off all the leaves and carefully remove the choke (the mass of silky hairs) by pulling it out with your fingers or scooping it out with a spoon. Immediately put the artichoke hearts in the acidulated water to prevent discoloration.

Cook the artichoke hearts in a pan of boiling salted water for 15 minutes, or until tender but still firm, then drain well and pat dry with paper towels.

Heat enough sunflower or olive oil in a deep-fat fryer to 350–375°F/ 180–190°C, or until a cube of bread browns in 30 seconds. Spear an artichoke heart on a toothpick and dip into the batter, then drop the artichoke heart and toothpick into the hot oil. Cook the artichoke hearts, in batches to avoid overcrowding, for 1–2 minutes, or until golden brown and crisp. Remove with a slotted spoon or draining basket and drain on paper towels.

Serve hot, accompanied by a bowl of aïoli for dipping.

marinated eggplants

SERVES 4
as part of a tapas meal

2 eggplants, halved lengthwise
salt and pepper
4 tbsp Spanish olive oil
2 garlic cloves, finely chopped
2 tbsp chopped fresh parsley
1 tbsp chopped fresh thyme
2 tbsp lemon juice

Make 2–3 slashes in the flesh of the eggplant halves and place, cut-side down, in an ovenproof dish. Season to taste with salt and pepper, then pour over the olive oil and sprinkle with the garlic, parsley, and thyme. Cover and let marinate at room temperature for 2–3 hours.

Preheat the oven to 350°F/180°C. Uncover the dish and roast the eggplants in the preheated oven for 45 minutes. Remove the dish from the oven and turn the eggplants over. Baste with the cooking juices and sprinkle with the lemon juice. Return to the oven and cook for an additional 15 minutes.

Transfer the eggplants to serving plates. Spoon over the cooking juices and serve hot or warm.

pickled stuffed sweet peppers

Cut the cheese into pieces about ¹/₂ inch/1 cm long. Slit the sides of the sweet peppers and seed, if you like. Stuff the peppers with the cheese.

Arrange the stuffed peppers on serving plates. Sprinkle with the dill and season to taste with salt and pepper. Cover and chill until ready to serve.

**SERVES 6
as part of a tapas meal**

7 oz/200 g Cuajada cheese, Queso del Tietar or other fresh goat cheese
14 oz/400 g pickled sweet peppers or pimientos del piquillo, drained
1 tbsp finely chopped fresh dill
salt and pepper

stuffed cherry tomatoes

SERVES 8
as part of a tapas meal

24 cherry tomatoes

for the anchovy & olive filling
1³/₄ oz/50 g canned anchovy
    fillets in olive oil
8 pimiento-stuffed green
    Spanish olives, finely chopped
2 large hard-cooked eggs,
    finely chopped
pepper

for the crab mayonnaise filling
6 oz/175 g canned crabmeat,
    drained
4 tbsp mayonnaise
1 tbsp chopped fresh flat-leaf
    parsley
salt and pepper
paprika, for garnish

for the black olive &
caper filling
12 pitted black Spanish olives
3 tbsp capers
6 tbsp aïoli (see page 50)
salt and pepper

If necessary, cut and discard a very thin slice from the stem end of each tomato to make the bases flat and stable. Cut a thin slice from the smooth end of each cherry tomato and discard. Using a serrated knife or teaspoon, loosen the pulp and seeds of each and scoop out, discarding the flesh. Turn the scooped-out tomatoes upside down on paper towels and let drain for 5 minutes.

To make the anchovy and olive filling, drain the anchovies, reserving the olive oil for later, then chop finely and place in a bowl. Add the olives and hard-cooked eggs. Pour in a trickle of the reserved olive oil to moisten the mixture, then season with pepper. (Don't add salt to season, as the anchovies are salty.) Mix well together.

To make the crab mayonnaise filling, place the crabmeat, mayonnaise, and parsley in a bowl and mix well together. Season the filling to taste with salt and pepper. Sprinkle with paprika before serving.

To make the black olive and caper filling, place the olives and capers on paper towels to drain them well, then chop finely and place in a bowl. Add the aïoli and mix well together. Season the filling to taste with salt and pepper.

Fill a pastry bag fitted with a ³/₄-inch/2-cm plain tip with the filling of your choice and use to fill the hollow tomato shells. Store the cherry tomatoes in the refrigerator until ready to serve.

simmered summer vegetables

SERVES 6–8
as part of a tapas meal

1 large eggplant
4 tbsp Spanish olive oil
1 onion, thinly sliced
2 garlic cloves, finely chopped
2 zucchini, thinly sliced
1 red bell pepper, cored,
   seeded, and thinly sliced
1 green bell pepper, cored,
   seeded, and thinly sliced
8 tomatoes, peeled, seeded,
   and chopped
salt and pepper
chopped fresh flat-leaf parsley,
   for garnish
slices thick country bread,
   for serving (optional)

Cut the eggplant into 1-inch/2.5-cm cubes. Heat the oil in a large ovenproof casserole, then add the onion and cook over medium heat, stirring occasionally, for 5 minutes, or until softened but not browned. Add the garlic and cook, stirring, for 30 seconds, or until softened.

Increase the heat to medium-high, then add the eggplant cubes and cook, stirring occasionally, for 10 minutes, or until softened and beginning to brown. Add the zucchini and bell peppers and cook, stirring occasionally, for 10 minutes, or until softened. Add the tomatoes and season to taste with salt and pepper.

Bring the mixture to a boil, then reduce the heat, cover, and simmer, stirring occasionally so that the vegetables do not stick to the bottom of the pan, for 15–20 minutes, or until tender. If necessary, uncover, then increase the heat and cook to evaporate any excess liquid, as the mixture should be thick.

Serve hot or cold, garnished with chopped parsley and accompanied by bread slices, if using, for scooping up the vegetables.

fava beans with ham

Bring a large pan of salted water to a boil. Add the beans and continue to boil for 5–10 minutes until just tender. Drain and put in a bowl of cold water to stop further cooking. Unless the beans are young and tiny, peel off the outer skins.

Meanwhile, heat 1 tablespoon of the oil in a skillet over medium-high heat. Add the onion and cook for about 5 minutes until soft, but not brown. Add the beans.

Stir in the ham and parsley and check the seasoning; the meat is salty, so don't add salt until after tasting. Transfer to a serving bowl and drizzle with the remaining oil. Serve at room temperature with slices of French bread.

SERVES 4–6
as part of a tapas meal

1/2 cup fresh or frozen shelled
   fava beans
2 tbsp Spanish olive oil
1 Spanish red onion, chopped
   very finely
1 slice medium-thick Serrano
   ham or prosciutto, chopped
finely chopped fresh parsley,
   to taste
salt and pepper
French bread, for serving

baby leek & asparagus salad

SERVES 6
as part of a tapas meal

3 eggs
1 lb/450 g baby leeks, trimmed
8 oz/225 g fresh young
　asparagus spears, trimmed
2/3 cup mayonnaise
2 tbsp sherry vinegar
1 garlic clove, crushed
salt and pepper
2 tbsp capers

Put the eggs in a pan, then cover with cold water and slowly bring to a boil. Reduce the heat and simmer gently for 10 minutes. Immediately drain the eggs and rinse under cold running water to cool. Gently tap the eggs to crack the shells and let stand until cold.

Meanwhile, slice the leeks and asparagus into about 3 1/2-inch/9-cm lengths. Put both the vegetables in a pan of boiling water, then return to a boil and boil for 12 minutes, or until just tender. Drain and rinse under cold running water, then drain well.

Put the mayonnaise in a large bowl. Add the vinegar and garlic, then mix together until smooth. Season to taste with salt and pepper. Add the leeks and asparagus to the dressing and toss together until well coated. Transfer the vegetables to a serving dish, then cover and chill in the refrigerator for at least 1 hour.

Just before serving, crack the shells of the eggs all over and remove them. Slice the eggs into quarters and add to the salad. Sprinkle over the capers and serve.

zucchini salad
with cilantro dressing

SERVES 6
as part of a tapas meal

1 lb 2 oz/500 g small zucchini
1 tsp salt
1 tbsp Spanish olive oil
1 garlic clove, crushed
1/3 cup pine nuts

for the cilantro dressing
2 garlic cloves, chopped
1 tsp ground cumin
1/2 cup chopped fresh cilantro
  leaves
2 tbsp chopped fresh flat-leaf
  parsley
5 tbsp Spanish extra virgin
  olive oil
2 tbsp white wine vinegar
salt and pepper

Thinly slice the zucchini lengthwise. Layer the slices in a colander, sprinkling over a little salt, and set over a large plate. Let drain for about 1 hour.

Meanwhile, make the dressing. Put the garlic, cumin, and herbs in a food processor and pulse until well mixed.

With the motor running, add 1 tablespoon of the extra virgin olive oil, drop by drop. Using a spatula, scrape down the side of the bowl. With the motor running again, very slowly add the remaining oil in a thin, steady stream until it has all been incorporated and the dressing has slightly thickened. Add the vinegar to the dressing and process for 1 minute, or until blended. Season to taste with salt and pepper.

When the zucchini have drained, quickly rinse the slices under cold running water, then dry well with paper towels or a clean kitchen towel. Put in a large bowl and add the olive oil and garlic, then toss together lightly.

Heat a ridged grill pan. Add the zucchini slices, in batches in a single layer, and cook, turning once, for 5 minutes, or until tender. Transfer to a large serving bowl. Set aside and let cool slightly.

Sprinkle the pine nuts over the zucchini. If the dressing has separated, whisk it together, then drizzle some over the zucchini. Serve the zucchini accompanied by the remaining dressing in a small serving bowl.

summer salad in a tomato dressing

Put the eggs in a pan, then cover with cold water and slowly bring to a boil. Reduce the heat and simmer gently for 10 minutes. Immediately drain the eggs and rinse under cold running water to cool. Gently tap the eggs to crack the shells and let stand until cold.

Meanwhile, cut the beans into 1-inch/2.5-cm lengths. Cook in a pan of boiling water for 2 minutes, then drain well. Rinse under cold running water and let stand until cold.

To make the dressing, coarsely grate the tomatoes into a food processor, discarding the skins left in your hands. Add the garlic, oil, vinegar, paprika, and sugar and process until smooth. Season to taste with salt.

Put the cooled beans in a large serving bowl. Add the tomatoes and bell peppers and toss the vegetables together. Drizzle the dressing over the vegetables.

Sprinkle the gherkins, olives, and capers into the salad. Just before serving, crack the shells of the eggs all over and remove them. Slice the eggs into quarters and add to the salad.

SERVES 8
as part of a tapas meal

4 eggs
3 1/2 oz/100 g fine green beans
1 lb 2 oz/500 g cherry or baby
    plum tomatoes
1 green bell pepper, cored,
    seeded, and diced
1 yellow bell pepper, cored,
    seeded, and diced
4 small gherkins, sliced
heaping 1/4 cup pitted black
    Spanish olives, halved
1 tsp capers

for the tomato dressing
6 firm tomatoes
1 garlic clove, chopped
6 tbsp Spanish extra virgin
    olive oil
3 tbsp sherry vinegar
1/2 tsp hot or sweet smoked
    Spanish paprika
pinch of sugar
salt

roasted bell pepper salad

SERVES 8
as part of a tapas meal

3 red bell peppers
3 yellow bell peppers
5 tbsp Spanish extra virgin
   olive oil
2 tbsp dry sherry vinegar or
   lemon juice
2 garlic cloves, crushed
pinch of sugar
salt and pepper
1 tbsp capers
8 small black Spanish olives
2 tbsp chopped fresh marjoram,
   plus extra sprigs for garnish

Preheat the broiler. Place all the bell peppers on a wire rack or broiler pan and cook under a hot broiler for 10 minutes, turning them frequently, until their skins have blackened and blistered.

Remove the roasted bell peppers from the heat, then place them in a bowl and immediately cover tightly with a clean, damp dish towel. Alternatively, place the bell peppers in a plastic bag. You will find that the steam helps to soften the skins and makes it easier to remove them. Let the bell peppers stand for about 15 minutes, or until they are cool enough to handle.

Holding 1 bell pepper at a time over a clean bowl, use a sharp knife to make a small hole in the base and gently squeeze out the juices and reserve them. Still holding the bell pepper over the bowl, carefully peel off the skin with your fingers or a knife and discard it. Cut the bell peppers in half and remove the stem, core, and seeds, then cut each bell pepper into neat thin strips. Arrange the bell pepper strips attractively on a serving dish.

Add the olive oil, sherry vinegar, garlic, sugar, and salt and pepper to taste to the reserved pepper juices. Whisk together until combined, then drizzle the dressing over the salad.

Sprinkle the capers, olives, and chopped marjoram over the salad, then garnish with marjoram sprigs and serve at room temperature.

orange & fennel salad

SERVES 4
as part of a tapas meal

4 large, juicy oranges
1 large fennel bulb, very thinly
  sliced
1 mild white onion, finely sliced
2 tbsp Spanish extra virgin
  olive oil
12 plump black Spanish olives,
  pitted and thinly sliced
1 fresh red chile, seeded and
  very thinly sliced (optional)
finely chopped fresh parsley
French bread, for serving

Finely grate the rind from the oranges into a bowl and reserve. Using a small, serrated knife, remove all the white pith from the oranges, working over a bowl to catch the juices. Cut the oranges horizontally into thin slices.

Toss the orange slices with the fennel and onion slices. Whisk the olive oil into the reserved orange juice, then spoon over the oranges. Sprinkle the olive slices over the top, add the chile, if using, then sprinkle with the orange rind and parsley. Serve with slices of French bread.

patatas bravas

To make the sauce, heat 2 tablespoons of oil in a pan, then add the onion and cook over medium heat, stirring occasionally, for 5 minutes, or until softened but not browned. Add the garlic and cook, stirring, for 30 seconds. Add the wine and bring to a boil. Add the tomatoes, vinegar, chiles, and paprika, then reduce the heat and simmer, uncovered, for 10–15 minutes, or until a thick sauce forms.

When the sauce is cooked, use a handheld blender to blend until smooth. Alternatively, transfer the sauce to a food processor and process until smooth. Return the sauce to the pan and set aside.

Do not peel the potatoes, but cut them into chunky pieces. Heat enough oil in a large skillet to come about 1 inch/2.5 cm up the side of the skillet. Add the potato pieces and cook over medium-high heat, turning occasionally, for 10–15 minutes until golden brown. Remove with a slotted spoon and drain on paper towels, then sprinkle with salt.

Meanwhile, gently reheat the sauce. Transfer the potatoes to a warmed serving dish and drizzle over the sauce. Serve hot, with wooden toothpicks to spear the potatoes.

SERVES 6
as part of a tapas meal

Spanish olive oil, for pan-frying
1 onion, finely chopped
2 garlic cloves, crushed
1/4 cup white wine or dry
   Spanish sherry
14 oz/400 g canned chopped
   tomatoes
2 tsp white or red wine vinegar
1–2 tsp crushed dried chiles
2 tsp hot or sweet smoked
   Spanish paprika
2 lb 4 oz/1 kg potatoes
salt

baby potatoes
with aïoli

SERVES 6–8
as part of a tapas meal

1 lb/450 g baby new potatoes
1 tbsp chopped fresh flat-leaf
  parsley
salt

for the aïoli
1 large egg yolk, at room
  temperature
1 tbsp white wine vinegar or
  lemon juice
2 large garlic cloves, peeled
salt and pepper
5 tbsp Spanish extra virgin
  olive oil
5 tbsp corn oil

To make the aïoli, place the egg yolk, vinegar, garlic, and salt and pepper to taste in a food processor fitted with a metal blade and blend together. With the motor still running, very slowly add the olive oil, then the corn oil, drop by drop at first, then, when it begins to thicken, in a slow, steady stream until the sauce is thick and smooth. Alternatively, use a bowl and whisk to make the aïoli.

For this recipe, the aïoli should be quite thin to coat the potatoes. To ensure this, blend in 1 tablespoon of water to form the consistency of sauce.

To prepare the potatoes, cut them in half or quarters to make bite-size pieces. If they are very small you can leave them whole. Place the potatoes in a large pan of cold salted water and bring to a boil. Reduce the heat and simmer for 7 minutes, or until just tender. Drain well, then transfer to a large bowl.

While the potatoes are still warm, pour over the aïoli sauce and gently toss the potatoes in it. Adding the sauce to the potatoes while they are still warm will help them to absorb the garlic flavor. Let stand for 20 minutes so that the potatoes marinate in the sauce.

Transfer the potatoes with aïoli to a warmed serving dish. Sprinkle over the parsley and salt to taste and serve warm. Alternatively, the dish can be prepared ahead and stored in the refrigerator, but return it to room temperature before serving.

potato wedges
with shallots & rosemary

SERVES 6
as part of a tapas meal

2 lb 4 oz/1 kg small potatoes
6 tbsp Spanish olive oil
2 fresh rosemary sprigs
5^1/$_2$ oz/150 g baby shallots
2 garlic cloves, sliced
salt and pepper

Preheat the oven to 400°F/200°C. Peel and cut each potato into 8 thick wedges. Put the potatoes in a large pan of salted water and bring to a boil. Reduce the heat and simmer for 5 minutes.

Heat the oil in a large roasting pan on the stove. Drain the potatoes well and add to the roasting pan. Strip the leaves off the rosemary sprigs, then finely chop and sprinkle over the potatoes.

Roast the potatoes in the preheated oven for 35 minutes, turning twice during cooking. Add the shallots and garlic and roast for an additional 15 minutes, or until golden brown. Season to taste with salt and pepper.

Transfer to a warmed serving dish and serve hot.

meat & poultry

As Spain is a country of serious carnivores, many meat and chicken tapas are popular. The country's seemingly infinite variety of highly prized cured hams and sausages are ideal for tapas in a hurry, as a sandwich filling, or chopped and used to flavor Crispy Chicken & Ham Croquettes.

When you want a tapas that is more than just one bite, take a look at the recipes in this chapter. Moroccan Chicken Kabobs, Beef Skewers with Orange & Garlic, and Lamb Skewers with Lemon are examples of *pinchos*, tapas cooked on small wooden skewers, eliminating the need for knives or forks. Or, try Porterhouse Steak with Garlic & Sherry or Sautéed Chicken with Crispy Garlic Slices.

porterhouse steak
with garlic & sherry

SERVES 6–8
as part of a tapas meal

4 porterhouse steaks, about
   6–8 oz/175–225 g each
   and 1 inch/2.5 cm thick
5 garlic cloves
salt and pepper
3 tbsp Spanish olive oil
1/2 cup dry Spanish sherry
chopped fresh flat-leaf parsley,
   for garnish
crusty bread, for serving

Cut the steaks into 1-inch/2.5-cm cubes and put in a large, shallow dish. Slice 3 of the garlic cloves and set aside. Finely chop the remaining garlic cloves and sprinkle over the steak cubes. Season generously with pepper and mix together well. Cover and let marinate in the refrigerator for 1–2 hours.

Heat the oil in a large skillet, then add the garlic slices and cook over low heat, stirring, for 1 minute, or until golden brown. Increase the heat to medium-high, then add the steak cubes and cook, stirring constantly, for 2–3 minutes, or until browned and almost cooked to your liking.

Add the sherry and cook until it has evaporated slightly. Season to taste with salt and turn into a warmed serving dish. Garnish with chopped parsley and serve hot, accompanied by chunks or slices of crusty bread to mop up the juices.

beef skewers with orange & garlic

SERVES 6–8
as part of a tapas meal

3 tbsp white wine
2 tbsp Spanish olive oil
3 garlic cloves, finely chopped
juice of 1 orange
1 lb/450 g beef top round, cubed
salt and pepper
1 lb/450 g pearl onions, halved
2 orange bell peppers, seeded
    and cut into squares
8 oz/225 g cherry tomatoes,
    halved

Mix the wine, olive oil, garlic, and orange juice together in a shallow, nonmetallic dish. Add the cubes of beef, season to taste with salt and pepper, and toss to coat. Cover with plastic wrap and let marinate in the refrigerator for 2–8 hours.

Preheat the broiler to high. Drain the beef, reserving the marinade. Thread the beef, onions, bell peppers, and tomatoes alternately onto several small skewers.

Cook the skewers under the hot broiler, turning and brushing frequently with the marinade, for 10 minutes, or until cooked through. Transfer to warmed serving plates and serve immediately.

calves' liver in almond saffron sauce

To make the sauce, heat 2 tablespoons of the oil in a large skillet. Tear the bread into small pieces and add to the skillet with the almonds. Cook over low heat, stirring frequently, for 2 minutes, or until golden brown. Stir in the garlic and cook, stirring, for 30 seconds.

Add the saffron and sherry to the skillet and season to taste with salt and pepper. Bring to a boil and continue to boil for 1–2 minutes. Remove from the heat and let cool slightly, then transfer the mixture to a food processor. Add the stock and process until smooth. Set aside.

Cut the liver into large bite-size pieces. Dust lightly with flour and season generously with pepper. Heat the remaining oil in the skillet, then add the liver and cook over medium heat, stirring constantly, for 2–3 minutes, or until firm and lightly browned.

Pour the sauce into the skillet and reheat gently for 1–2 minutes. Transfer to a warmed serving dish and garnish with chopped parsley. Serve hot, accompanied by chunks of crusty bread to mop up the sauce.

SERVES 6
as part of a tapas meal

4 tbsp Spanish olive oil
1 oz/25 g white bread
2/3 cup blanched almonds
2 garlic cloves, crushed
pinch of saffron strands
2/3 cup dry Spanish sherry
   or white wine
salt and pepper
1 1/4 cups vegetable stock
1 lb/450 g calves' liver
all-purpose flour, for dusting
chopped fresh flat-leaf parsley,
   for garnish
crusty bread, for serving

lamb skewers
with lemon

SERVES 8
as part of a tapas meal

2 garlic cloves, finely chopped
1 Spanish onion, finely chopped
2 tsp finely grated lemon rind
2 tbsp lemon juice
1 tsp fresh thyme leaves
1 tsp ground coriander
1 tsp ground cumin
2 tbsp red wine vinegar
1/2 cup Spanish olive oil
2 lb 4 oz/1 kg lamb fillet,
   cut into 3/4-inch/2-cm pieces
orange or lemon slices,
   for garnish

Mix the garlic, onion, lemon rind, lemon juice, thyme, coriander, cumin, vinegar, and olive oil together in a large, shallow, nonmetallic dish, whisking well until thoroughly combined.

Thread the pieces of lamb onto 16 wooden skewers and add to the dish, turning well to coat. Cover with plastic wrap and let marinate in the refrigerator for 2–8 hours, turning occasionally.

Preheat the broiler to medium. Drain the skewers, reserving the marinade. Cook under the hot broiler, turning frequently and brushing with the marinade, for 10 minutes, or until tender and cooked to your liking.

Serve immediately, garnished with orange or lemon slices.

tiny meatballs
in almond sauce

SERVES 6–8
as part of a tapas meal

2 oz/55 g white or brown bread,
    crusts removed
3 tbsp water
1 lb/450 g fresh ground lean
    pork, beef, or lamb
1 large onion, finely chopped
1 garlic clove, crushed
2 tbsp chopped fresh flat-leaf
    parsley, plus extra to garnish
1 egg, beaten
freshly grated nutmeg
salt and pepper
all-purpose flour, for coating
2 tbsp Spanish olive oil
lemon juice, to taste
crusty bread, for serving

for the almond sauce
2 tbsp Spanish olive oil
1 oz/25 g white or brown bread
4 oz/115 g blanched almonds
2 garlic cloves, finely chopped
2/3 cup dry white wine
salt and pepper
1 3/4 cups vegetable stock

To prepare the meatballs, place the bread in a bowl, then add the water and let soak for 5 minutes. With your hands, squeeze out the water and return the bread to a dry bowl. Add the ground meat, onion, garlic, parsley, and egg, then season with grated nutmeg and a little salt and pepper. Knead the ingredients well to form a smooth mixture.

Spread some flour on a plate. With floured hands, shape the meat mixture into about 30 equal-size balls, then roll each meatball again in flour until coated.

Heat the olive oil in a large, heavy-bottom skillet. Add the meatballs, in batches, and cook for 4–5 minutes, or until browned on all sides. Using a slotted spoon, remove the meatballs from the skillet and reserve.

To make the sauce, heat the olive oil in the same skillet in which the meatballs were fried. Break the bread into pieces, then add to the skillet with the almonds and cook gently, stirring frequently, until the bread and almonds are golden brown. Add the garlic and fry for an additional 30 seconds, then pour in the wine and boil for 1–2 minutes. Season to taste with salt and pepper and let cool slightly.

Transfer the almond mixture to a food processor. Pour in the vegetable stock and process the mixture until smooth. Return the sauce to the skillet.

Carefully add the meatballs to the almond sauce and simmer for 25 minutes, or until the meatballs are tender. Taste the sauce and season with salt and pepper if necessary.

Transfer the cooked meatballs and sauce to a warmed serving dish, then add a squeeze of lemon juice to taste and sprinkle with chopped parsley for garnish. Serve piping hot with crusty bread for mopping up the almond sauce.

spanish meatballs
with cracked olives

Put the bread in a bowl, then add the water and let soak for 5 minutes. Using your hands, squeeze out as much of the water as possible from the bread and put the bread in a clean bowl.

Add the ground meat, 1 chopped onion, 2 crushed garlic cloves, the cumin, coriander, and egg to the bread. Season to taste with salt and, using your hands, mix together well. Dust a plate or cookie sheet with flour. Using floured hands, roll the mixture into 30 equal-size, small balls, then put on the plate or cookie sheet and roll lightly in the flour.

Heat 2 tablespoons of the oil in a large skillet, then add the meatballs, in batches to avoid overcrowding, and cook over medium heat, turning frequently, for 8–10 minutes, until golden brown on all sides and firm. Remove with a slotted spoon and set aside.

Heat the remaining oil in the skillet, then add the remaining onion and cook, stirring occasionally, for 5 minutes, or until softened but not browned. Add the remaining garlic and cook, stirring, for 30 seconds. Add the tomatoes, sherry, paprika, and sugar and season to taste with salt. Bring to a boil, then reduce the heat and simmer for 10 minutes.

Using a handheld blender, blend the tomato mixture until smooth. Alternatively, turn the tomato mixture into a food processor or blender and process until smooth. Return the sauce to the pan.

Carefully return the meatballs to the skillet and add the olives. Simmer gently for 20 minutes, or until the meatballs are tender. Serve hot, with crusty bread to mop up the sauce.

SERVES 6
as part of a tapas meal

2 oz/55 g day-old bread, crusts removed
3 tbsp water
1 1/8 cups lean fresh ground pork
1 1/8 cups lean fresh ground lamb
2 small onions, finely chopped
3 garlic cloves, crushed
1 tsp ground cumin
1 tsp ground coriander
1 egg, lightly beaten
salt
all-purpose flour, for dusting
3 tbsp Spanish olive oil
14 oz/400 g canned chopped tomatoes
5 tbsp dry sherry or red wine
pinch of hot or sweet smoked Spanish paprika
pinch of sugar
1 cup cracked green Spanish olives in extra virgin olive oil
crusty bread, for serving

spareribs coated in paprika sauce

SERVES 6
as part of a tapas meal

Spanish olive oil, for oiling
2 lb 12 oz/1.25 kg pork
  spareribs
1/3 cup dry Spanish sherry
5 tsp hot or sweet smoked
  Spanish paprika
2 garlic cloves, crushed
1 tbsp dried oregano
2/3 cup water
salt

Preheat the oven to 425°F/220°C. Oil a large roasting pan. If the butcher has not already done so, cut the sheets of spareribs into individual ribs. If possible, cut each sparerib in half widthwise. Put the spareribs in the prepared pan, in a single layer, and roast in the preheated oven for 20 minutes.

Meanwhile, make the sauce. Put the sherry, paprika, garlic, oregano, water, and salt to taste in a pitcher and mix together well.

Reduce the oven temperature to 350°F/180°C. Pour off the fat from the pan, then pour the sauce over the spareribs and turn the spareribs to coat with the sauce on both sides. Roast for an additional 45 minutes, basting the spareribs with the sauce once halfway through the cooking time, until tender.

Pile the spareribs into a warmed serving dish. Bring the sauce in the roasting pan to a boil on the stove, then reduce the heat and simmer until reduced by half. Pour the sauce over the spareribs and serve hot.

miniature pork brochettes

SERVES 4–6
as part of a tapas meal

1 lb/450 g lean, boneless pork
3 tbsp Spanish olive oil,
  plus extra for oiling (optional)
grated rind and juice of
  1 large lemon
2 garlic cloves, crushed
2 tbsp chopped fresh flat-leaf
  parsley, plus extra for garnish
1 tbsp ras-el-hanout spice blend
salt and pepper

The brochettes are marinated overnight, so remember to do this in advance in order that they are ready when you need them. Cut the pork into pieces about $3/4$ inch/2 cm square and put in a large, shallow, nonmetallic dish that will hold the pieces in a single layer.

To prepare the marinade, place all the remaining ingredients in a bowl and mix together. Pour the marinade over the pork and toss the meat in it until well coated. Cover the dish and let marinate in the refrigerator for 8 hours or overnight, stirring the pork 2–3 times.

You can use wooden or metal skewers to cook the brochettes and for this recipe you will need about 12 x 6-inch/15-cm skewers. If you are using wooden ones, soak them in cold water for 30 minutes prior to using. Metal skewers simply need to be greased.

Preheat the broiler or grill pan. Thread 3 marinated pork pieces, leaving a little space between each piece, onto each prepared skewer. Cook the brochettes for 10–15 minutes, or until tender and lightly charred, turning several times and basting with the remaining marinade during cooking. Serve the pork brochettes piping hot, garnished with parsley.

serrano ham croquettes

Heat the olive oil in a pan, then add the onion and cook over medium heat, stirring occasionally, for 5 minutes, or until softened but not browned. Add the garlic and cook, stirring, for 30 seconds. Stir in the flour and cook over low heat, stirring constantly, for 1 minute without the mixture coloring.

Remove the pan from the heat and gradually stir in the milk to form a smooth sauce. Return to the heat and slowly bring to a boil, stirring constantly, until the sauce boils and thickens.

Remove the pan from the heat, then stir in the ham and paprika and season to taste with salt. Spread the mixture in a shallow dish and let cool, then cover and chill in the refrigerator for at least 2 hours or overnight.

When the mixture has chilled, break the egg onto a plate and beat lightly. Spread the breadcrumbs on a separate plate. Using wet hands, form the ham mixture into 8 even-size pieces and form each piece into a cylindrical shape. Dip the croquettes, one at a time, into the beaten egg, then roll in the breadcrumbs to coat. Put on a plate and chill in the refrigerator for at least 1 hour.

Heat enough sunflower oil for deep-frying in a deep-fat fryer to 350–375°F/180–190°C, or until a cube of bread browns in 30 seconds. Add the croquettes, in batches to avoid overcrowding, and cook for 5 minutes, or until golden brown and crisp. Remove with a slotted spoon or draining basket and drain on paper towels. Keep hot in a warm oven while you cook the remaining croquettes. Serve hot with aïoli.

SERVES 4
as part of a tapas meal

4 tbsp Spanish olive oil
1 small onion, finely chopped
1 garlic clove, crushed
4 tbsp all-purpose flour
scant 1 cup milk
7 oz/200 g Serrano ham or cooked ham, in one piece, finely diced
pinch of hot or sweet smoked Spanish paprika
salt
1 egg
1 cup day-old white breadcrumbs
sunflower oil, for deep-frying
aïoli (see page 50), for serving

empanadillas with ham & goat cheese

SERVES 16
as part of a tapas meal

1 tbsp Spanish olive oil
1 small onion, finely chopped
1 garlic clove, crushed
5¹/2 oz/150 g soft goat cheese
6 oz/175 g thickly sliced cooked
    ham, finely chopped
scant ¹/2 cup capers, chopped
¹/2 tsp hot or sweet smoked
    Spanish paprika
salt
1 lb 2 oz/500 g prepared puff
    pastry, thawed if frozen
all-purpose flour, for dusting
beaten egg, for glazing

Preheat the oven to 400°F/200°C. Dampen several large cookie sheets. Heat the oil in a large skillet, then add the onion and cook over medium heat, stirring occasionally, for 5 minutes, or until softened but not browned. Add the garlic and cook, stirring, for 30 seconds.

Put the goat cheese in a bowl, then add the ham, capers, onion mixture, and paprika and mix together well. Season to taste with salt.

Thinly roll out the pastry on a lightly floured counter. Using a plain, 3¹/4-inch/8-cm round cutter, cut out 32 circles, rerolling the trimmings as necessary. Using a teaspoon, put an equal, small amount of the goat cheese mixture in the center of each pastry circle. Dampen the edges of the pastry with a little water and fold one half over the other to form a crescent and enclose the filling. Pinch the edges together with your fingers to seal, then press with the tines of a fork to seal further. Transfer to the prepared cookie sheets.

With the tip of a sharp knife, make a small slit in the top of each pastry and brush with beaten egg to glaze. Bake in the preheated oven for 15 minutes, or until risen and golden brown. Serve warm.

chorizo in red wine

SERVES 6
as part of a tapas meal

7 oz/200 g chorizo sausage
³/₄ cup Spanish red wine
2 tbsp brandy (optional)
fresh flat-leaf parsley sprigs,
    for garnish
crusty bread, for serving

Before you begin, bear in mind that this dish is best if prepared the day before you are planning to serve it. Using a fork, prick the chorizo in 3 or 4 places. Place the chorizo and wine in a large pan. Bring the wine to a boil, then reduce the heat and simmer gently, covered, for 15–20 minutes. Transfer the chorizo and wine to a bowl or dish, cover and let the sausage marinate in the wine for 8 hours or overnight.

The next day, remove the chorizo from the bowl or dish and reserve the wine. Remove the outer casing from the chorizo and cut the sausage into ¹/₄-inch/5-mm slices. Place the slices in a large, heavy-bottom skillet or flameproof serving dish.

If you are adding the brandy, pour it into a small pan and heat gently. Pour the brandy over the chorizo slices, then stand well back and set aflame. When the flames have died down, shake the pan gently and add the reserved wine to the pan, then cook over high heat until almost all of the wine has evaporated.

Serve the chorizo in red wine piping hot, in the dish in which it was cooked, sprinkled with parsley to garnish. Accompany with chunks or slices of bread to mop up the juices and provide wooden toothpicks to spear the pieces of chorizo.

chickpeas & chorizo

Cut the chorizo into $^1/_2$-inch/1-cm dice. Heat the oil in a heavy-bottom skillet over medium heat, then add the onion and garlic. Cook, stirring occasionally, until the onion is softened but not browned. Stir in the chorizo and cook until heated through.

Transfer the mixture to a bowl and stir in the chickpeas and pimientos. Splash with sherry vinegar and season to taste with salt and pepper. Serve hot or at room temperature, generously sprinkled with parsley, with plenty of crusty bread.

**SERVES 4–6
as part of a tapas meal**

9 oz/250 g chorizo sausage in
   1 piece, outer casing removed
4 tbsp Spanish olive oil
1 onion, finely chopped
1 large garlic clove, crushed
14 oz/400 g canned chickpeas,
   drained and rinsed
6 pimientos del piquillo, drained,
   patted dry, and sliced
1 tbsp sherry vinegar, or to taste
salt and pepper
finely chopped fresh parsley,
   for garnish
crusty bread slices, for serving

chorizo & mushroom kabobs

SERVES 8
as part of a tapas meal

2 tbsp Spanish olive oil
24 slices chorizo sausage, each
    about 1/2 inch/1 cm thick
    (about 31/2 oz/100 g)
24 button mushrooms, wiped
1 green bell pepper, roasted,
    peeled, and cut into
    24 squares

Heat the olive oil in a skillet over medium heat. Add the chorizo and cook for 20 seconds, stirring.

Add the mushrooms and continue cooking for an additional 1–2 minutes until the mushrooms begin to brown and absorb the fat in the skillet.

Thread a bell pepper square, a piece of chorizo, and a mushroom onto a wooden toothpick. Continue until all the ingredients are used. Serve hot or at room temperature.

crispy chicken
& ham croquettes

SERVES 4
as part of a tapas meal

4 tbsp Spanish olive oil or
    butter
4 tbsp all-purpose flour
3/4 cup milk
4 oz/115 g cooked chicken,
    ground
2 oz/55 g Serrano or cooked
    ham, very finely chopped
1 tbsp chopped fresh flat-leaf
    parsley
small pinch of freshly grated
    nutmeg
salt and pepper
1 egg, beaten
1 cup day-old white
    breadcrumbs
corn oil, for deep-frying
aïoli (see page 50), for serving

Heat the olive oil or butter in a pan. Stir in the flour to form a paste and cook gently for 1 minute, stirring constantly. Remove the pan from the heat and gradually stir in the milk until smooth. Return to the heat and slowly bring to a boil, stirring constantly, until the mixture thickens.

Remove the pan from the heat, add the ground chicken and beat until the mixture is smooth. Add the chopped ham, parsley, and nutmeg and mix well. Season the mixture to taste with salt and pepper. Spread the chicken mixture in a dish and let stand for 30 minutes until cool, then cover and let chill for 2–3 hours or overnight. Don't be tempted to skip this stage, as chilling the croquettes helps to stop them falling apart when they are cooked.

When the chicken mixture has chilled, pour the beaten egg onto a plate and spread the breadcrumbs out on a separate plate. Divide the chicken mixture into 8 equal-size portions. With dampened hands, form each portion into a cylindrical shape. Dip the croquettes, one at a time, in the beaten egg, then roll in the breadcrumbs to coat them. Place on a plate and let chill for 1 hour.

To cook, heat the corn oil in a deep-fat fryer to 350–375°F/180–190°C, or until a cube of bread browns in 30 seconds. Add the croquettes, in batches to prevent the temperature of the oil from dropping, and deep-fry for 5–10 minutes, or until golden brown and crispy. Remove with a slotted spoon and drain well on paper towels.

Serve the chicken and ham croquettes piping hot, accompanied by a bowl of aïoli for dipping.

sautéed chicken
with crispy garlic slices

If necessary, halve the chicken thighs and remove the bones, then cut the flesh into bite-size pieces, leaving the skin on. Season to taste with paprika.

Heat the oil in a large skillet or an ovenproof casserole, then add the garlic slices and cook over medium heat, stirring frequently, for 1 minute, or until golden brown. Remove with a slotted spoon and drain on paper towels.

Add the chicken thighs to the skillet and cook, turning occasionally, for 10 minutes, or until tender and golden brown on all sides. Add the wine and bay leaf and bring to a boil. Reduce the heat and simmer, stirring occasionally, for 10 minutes, or until most of the liquid has evaporated and the juices run clear when a skewer is inserted into the thickest part of the meat. Season to taste with salt.

Transfer the chicken to a warmed serving dish and sprinkle over the reserved garlic slices. Sprinkle with chopped parsley for garnish and serve with chunks of crusty bread to mop up the juices, if using.

SERVES 8
as part of a tapas meal

8 skin-on chicken thighs,
 boned if available
hot or sweet smoked Spanish
 paprika, to taste
4 tbsp Spanish olive oil
10 garlic cloves, sliced
1/2 cup dry white wine
1 bay leaf
salt
chopped fresh flat-leaf parsley,
 for garnish
crusty bread, for serving
 (optional)

chicken rolls with olives

SERVES 6–8
as part of a tapas meal

²/₃ cup black Spanish olives in
oil, drained and 2 tbsp oil
reserved
²/₃ cup butter, softened
4 tbsp chopped fresh parsley
4 skinless, boneless chicken
breasts

Preheat the oven to 400°F/200°C. Pit and finely chop the olives. Mix the olives, butter, and parsley together in a bowl.

Place the chicken breasts between 2 sheets of plastic wrap and beat gently with a meat mallet or the side of a rolling pin.

Spread the olive and herb butter over one side of each flattened chicken breast and roll up. Secure with a wooden toothpick or tie with clean string if necessary.

Place the chicken rolls in an ovenproof dish. Drizzle over the oil from the olive jar and bake in the preheated oven for 45–55 minutes, or until tender and the juices run clear when the chicken is pierced with the point of a sharp knife.

Transfer the chicken rolls to a cutting board and discard the toothpicks or string. Using a sharp knife, cut into slices, then transfer to warmed serving plates and serve.

moroccan chicken kabobs

SERVES 4
as part of a tapas meal

1 lb/450 g chicken breast fillets
3 tbsp Spanish olive oil,
   plus extra for oiling
juice of 1 lemon
2 garlic cloves, crushed
1$\frac{1}{2}$ tsp ground cumin
1 tsp ground coriander
1 tsp hot or sweet smoked
   Spanish paprika
$\frac{1}{4}$ tsp ground cinnamon
$\frac{1}{2}$ tsp dried oregano
salt
chopped fresh flat-leaf parsley,
   for garnish

Cut the chicken into 1-inch/2.5-cm cubes and put in a large, shallow, nonmetallic dish. Put all the remaining ingredients, except the parsley, in a bowl and whisk together. Pour the marinade over the chicken cubes and toss the meat in the marinade until well coated. Cover and let marinate in the refrigerator for 8 hours or overnight, turning the chicken 2–3 times if possible.

  If using wooden skewers or toothpicks, soak the skewers in cold water for about 30 minutes to help prevent them from burning and the food sticking to them during cooking. If using metal skewers, lightly brush with oil. Preheat the broiler or grill pan. Remove the chicken pieces from the marinade, reserving the remaining marinade, and thread an equal quantity onto each prepared skewer or toothpick, leaving a little space between each piece.

  Brush the broiler rack or grill pan with a little oil. Add the kabobs and cook, turning frequently and brushing with the reserved marinade halfway through cooking, for 15 minutes, or until browned on all sides, tender, and cooked through. Serve hot, sprinkled with chopped parsley to garnish.

chicken wings with tomato dressing

Preheat the oven to 350°F/180°C. Mix 1 tablespoon of the oil with the garlic and cumin in a shallow dish. Cut off and discard the tips of the chicken wings and add the wings to the spice mixture, turning to coat. Cover with plastic wrap and let marinate in a cool place for 15 minutes.

Heat 3 tablespoons of the remaining oil in a large, heavy-bottom skillet. Add the chicken wings, in batches, and cook, turning frequently, until golden brown. Transfer to a roasting pan.

Roast the chicken wings for 10–15 minutes, or until tender and the juices run clear when the point of a sharp knife is inserted into the thickest part of the meat.

Meanwhile, mix the remaining olive oil, the tomatoes, vinegar, and basil together in a bowl.

Using tongs, transfer the chicken wings to a nonmetallic dish. Pour the dressing over them, turning to coat. Cover with plastic wrap and let cool, then chill for 4 hours. Remove from the refrigerator 30–60 minutes before serving to return to room temperature.

SERVES 6–8
as part of a tapas meal

3/4 cup Spanish olive oil
3 garlic cloves, finely chopped
1 tsp ground cumin
2 lb 4 oz/1 kg chicken wings
2 tomatoes, peeled, seeded, and diced
5 tbsp white wine vinegar
1 tbsp shredded fresh basil leaves

chicken livers
in sherry sauce

SERVES 6
as part of a tapas meal

1 lb/450 g chicken livers
2 tbsp Spanish olive oil
1 small onion, finely chopped
2 garlic cloves, finely chopped
scant 1/2 cup dry Spanish sherry
salt and pepper
2 tbsp chopped fresh flat-leaf
    parsley, plus extra sprigs,
    for garnish
crusty bread or toast,
    for serving

If necessary, trim the livers, cutting away any ducts and gristle, then cut into small, bite-size pieces. Heat the oil in a large, heavy-bottom skillet. Add the onion and cook for 5 minutes, or until softened but not browned. Add the garlic and cook for an additional 30 seconds.

Add the livers to the skillet and cook for 2–3 minutes, stirring constantly, until they are firm and have changed color on the outside but are still pink and soft in the center. Using a slotted spoon, lift the livers from the skillet and transfer to a large, warmed serving dish or several smaller ones. Keep warm.

Add the sherry to the skillet, increase the heat, and let it bubble for 3–4 minutes to evaporate the alcohol and reduce slightly. At the same time, deglaze the skillet by scraping and stirring all the bits on the base of the skillet into the sauce with a wooden spoon. Season the sauce to taste with salt and pepper.

Pour the sherry sauce over the chicken livers and sprinkle over the parsley. Garnish with parsley sprigs and serve piping hot with chunks or slices of crusty bread or toast to mop up the sauce.

chicken salad
with raisins & pine nuts

SERVES 6–8
as part of a tapas meal

¹/₄ cup red wine vinegar
¹/₈ cup superfine sugar
1 bay leaf
pared rind of 1 lemon
scant 1 cup seedless raisins
4 large skinless, boneless
   chicken breasts, about
   1 lb 5 oz/600 g in total
5 tbsp Spanish olive oil
1 garlic clove, finely chopped
1 cup pine nuts
salt and pepper
¹/₃ cup Spanish extra virgin
   olive oil
1 small bunch of fresh flat-leaf
   parsley, finely chopped

To make the dressing, put the vinegar, sugar, bay leaf, and lemon rind in a pan and bring to a boil, then remove from the heat. Stir in the raisins and let cool.

When the dressing is cool, slice the chicken breasts widthwise into very thin slices. Heat the olive oil in a large skillet, then add the chicken slices and cook over medium heat, stirring occasionally, for 8–10 minutes, or until lightly browned and tender.

Add the garlic and pine nuts and cook, stirring constantly and shaking the skillet, for 1 minute, or until the pine nuts are golden brown. Season to taste with salt and pepper.

Pour the cooled dressing into a large bowl, discarding the bay leaf and lemon rind. Add the extra virgin olive oil and whisk together. Season to taste with salt and pepper. Add the chicken mixture and parsley and toss together. Turn the salad into a serving dish and serve warm or, if serving cold, cover and chill in the refrigerator for 2–3 hours before serving.

fish & seafood

With miles of coastline along the Atlantic Ocean and Mediterranean, Spanish

fishermen provide cooks with a wealth of fresh fish and shellfish, resulting in

wonderful seafood tapas, sometimes as simple as shelled shrimp on toothpicks.

Yet, even with such fresh choices, Spaniards retain a soft spot for salt cod,

once often the only choice of seafood before modern transportation, and Salt

Cod Fritters with Spinach are always popular.

This chapter contains recipes from all over the country, and land and sea come

together in Scallops with Serrano Ham and Rosemary Skewers with Monkfish

& Bacon. In the sunny south, Sizzling Chile Shrimp is the ubiquitous tapas.

salt cod fritters
with spinach

SERVES 16
as part of a tapas meal

9 oz/250 g dried salt cod in
   1 piece
1 cup all-purpose flour
1 tsp baking powder
1/4 tsp salt
1 large egg, lightly beaten
about 2/3 cup milk
2 lemon slices
2 fresh parsley sprigs
1 bay leaf
1/2 tbsp garlic-flavored olive oil
3 oz/85 g fresh baby spinach,
   rinsed
1/4 tsp smoked sweet, mild, or
   hot Spanish paprika, to taste
Spanish olive oil, for frying
coarse sea salt (optional)
aïoli (see page 50), for serving

Place the dried salt cod in a large bowl. Cover with cold water and let soak for 48 hours, changing the water at least 3 times a day.

Meanwhile, make the batter. Sift the flour, baking powder, and salt into a large bowl and make a well. Mix the egg with 1/2 cup of the milk and pour into the well in the flour, stirring to make a smooth batter with a thick coating consistency. If it seems too thick, gradually stir in the remaining milk, then let stand for at least 1 hour.

After the salt cod has soaked, transfer it to a large skillet. Add the lemon slices, parsley sprigs, bay leaf, and enough water to cover and bring to a boil. Reduce the heat and simmer for 30–45 minutes, or until the fish is tender and flakes easily.

Meanwhile, prepare the spinach. Heat the garlic-flavored olive oil in a small pan over medium heat. Add the spinach with just the water clinging to the leaves and cook for 3–4 minutes, or until wilted.

Drain the spinach in a strainer, using the back of a spoon to press out any excess moisture. Finely chop the spinach, then stir it into the batter with the paprika.

Remove the fish from the water and flake the flesh into pieces, removing all the skin and tiny bones. Stir the flesh into the batter.

Heat 2-inch/5-cm of olive oil in a heavy-bottom skillet to 350–375°F/180–190°C, or until a cube of bread browns in 30 seconds. Use a greased tablespoon or measuring spoon to drop spoonfuls of the batter into the oil, then cook for 8–10 minutes, or until golden brown. Work in batches to avoid crowding the skillet. Use a slotted spoon to transfer the fritters to paper towels to drain and sprinkle with sea salt, if using.

Serve hot or at room temperature with aïoli for dipping.

sardines with romesco sauce

SERVES 6
as part of a tapas meal

24 fresh sardines, scaled,
    cleaned, and heads removed
heaping ¾ cup all-purpose
    flour
4 eggs, lightly beaten
9 oz/250 g fresh white
    breadcrumbs
6 tbsp chopped fresh parsley
4 tbsp chopped fresh marjoram
vegetable oil, for deep-frying

for the romesco sauce
1 red bell pepper, halved and
    seeded
2 tomatoes, halved
4 garlic cloves
½ cup Spanish olive oil
1 slice white bread, diced
4 tbsp blanched almonds
1 fresh red chile, seeded and
    chopped
2 shallots, chopped
1 tsp paprika
2 tbsp red wine vinegar
2 tsp sugar
1 tbsp water

First make the sauce. Preheat the oven to 425°F/220°C. Place the bell pepper, tomatoes, and garlic in an ovenproof dish and drizzle over 1 tablespoon of the olive oil, turning to coat. Bake in the preheated oven for 20–25 minutes, then remove from the oven and cool. When cool enough to handle, peel off their skins and place the flesh in a food processor.

Heat 1 tablespoon of the remaining oil in a skillet. Add the bread and almonds and cook over low heat for a few minutes until browned. Remove and drain on paper towels. Add the chile, shallots, and paprika to the pan and cook for 5 minutes, or until the shallots are softened.

Transfer the almond mixture and shallot mixture to a food processor and add the vinegar, sugar, and water. Process to a paste. With the motor still running, gradually add the remaining oil through the feeder tube. Transfer to a bowl, cover, and reserve.

Place the sardines, skin-side up, on a cutting board and press along the length of the spines with your thumbs. Turn over and remove and discard the bones. Place the flour and eggs in separate bowls. Mix the breadcrumbs and herbs together in a third bowl. Toss the fish in the flour, the eggs, then in the breadcrumbs.

Heat the vegetable oil in a large pan to 350–375°F/180–190°C, or until a cube of bread browns in 30 seconds. Deep-fry the fish for 4–5 minutes, or until golden and tender. Drain and serve with the sauce.

fresh salmon with red bell pepper sauce

Preheat the oven to 400°F/200°C. Brush the red bell peppers with 2 teaspoons of the oil and put in a roasting pan. Roast in the preheated oven for 30 minutes, then turn over and roast for an additional 10 minutes, or until the skins have blistered and blackened.

Meanwhile, remove the skin from the salmon fillets and cut the flesh into 1-inch/2.5-cm cubes. Season to taste with pepper and set aside.

Heat 2 tablespoons of the remaining oil in a large skillet, then add the onion and cook, stirring occasionally, for 5 minutes, or until softened but not browned. Add the garlic and cook, stirring, for 30 seconds, or until softened. Add the wine and bring to a boil, then let bubble for 1 minute. Remove from the heat and set aside.

When the bell peppers are cooked, transfer to a plastic bag, using a slotted spoon, and let stand for 15 minutes, or until cool enough to handle. Using a sharp knife or your fingers, carefully peel away the skin from the bell peppers. Halve the bell peppers and remove the stems, cores, and seeds, then put the flesh in a food processor.

Add the onion mixture and cream to the bell peppers and process to a smooth purée. Season to taste with salt and pepper. Pour into a pan.

Heat the remaining oil in the skillet, then add the salmon cubes and cook, turning occasionally, for 8–10 minutes, or until cooked through and golden brown on both sides. Meanwhile, gently heat the sauce in the pan.

Transfer the cooked salmon to a warmed serving dish. Drizzle over some of the bell pepper sauce and serve the remaining sauce in a small serving bowl. Serve hot, garnished with chopped parsley and accompanied by crusty bread to mop up the sauce, if using.

SERVES 6
as part of a tapas meal

2 red bell peppers
about 4 tbsp Spanish olive oil
1 lb 9 oz/700 g salmon fillets
salt and pepper
1 onion, coarsely chopped
1 garlic clove, finely chopped
6 tbsp dry white wine
1/3 cup heavy cream
chopped fresh flat-leaf parsley,
    for garnish
crusty bread, for serving
    (optional)

rosemary skewers
with monkfish & bacon

SERVES 12
as part of a tapas meal

12 oz/350 g monkfish tail or
  9 oz/250 g monkfish fillet
12 fresh rosemary stems
3 tbsp Spanish olive oil
juice of 1/2 small lemon
1 garlic clove, crushed
salt and pepper
6 thick strips Canadian bacon
lemon wedges, for garnish
aïoli (see page 50), for serving

If using monkfish tail, cut either side of the central bone with a sharp knife and remove the flesh to form 2 fillets. Slice the fillets in half lengthwise, then cut each fillet into 12 bite-size chunks to give a total of 24 pieces. Place the monkfish pieces in a large bowl.

To prepare the rosemary skewers, strip the leaves off the stems and reserve them, leaving a few leaves at one end. For the marinade, finely chop the reserved leaves and whisk together in a bowl with the olive oil, lemon juice, garlic, and salt and pepper to taste. Add the monkfish pieces and toss until coated in the marinade. Cover and let marinate in the refrigerator for 1–2 hours.

Cut each bacon strip in half lengthwise, then in half widthwise, and roll up each piece. Thread 2 pieces of monkfish alternately with 2 bacon rolls onto each of the prepared rosemary skewers.

Preheat the broiler. Broil the skewers for 10 minutes, turning occasionally and basting with any remaining marinade, or until cooked. Serve hot, garnished with lemon wedges for squeezing over them and accompanied by a small bowl of aïoli in which to dip the monkfish skewers.

mixed seafood kabobs
with a chili & lime glaze

SERVES 4
as part of a tapas meal

16 raw jumbo shrimp, in their
  shells
12 oz/350 g monkfish or hake
  fillet
12 oz/350 g salmon fillet,
  skinned
1-inch/2.5-cm piece fresh
  ginger
4 tbsp sweet chili sauce
grated rind and juice of 1 lime
sunflower or Spanish olive oil,
  for oiling (optional)
lime wedges, for serving

Pull off the heads of the shrimp. With your fingers, peel away the shells, leaving the tails intact. Using a sharp knife, make a shallow slit along the length of the back of each shrimp, then use the tip of the knife to lift out the dark vein and discard. Rinse the shrimp under cold running water and pat dry with paper towels. Cut the monkfish and salmon into 1-inch/2.5-cm pieces.

Grate the ginger into a strainer set over a large, nonmetallic bowl to catch the juice. Squeeze the grated ginger to extract all the juice and discard the pulp.

Add the chili sauce and lime rind and juice to the ginger juice and mix together. Add the prepared seafood and stir to coat in the marinade. Cover and let marinate in the refrigerator for 30 minutes.

Meanwhile, if using wooden skewers, soak 8 in cold water for about 30 minutes to help prevent them from burning and the food sticking to them during cooking. If using metal skewers, lightly brush with oil.

Preheat the broiler to high and line the broiler pan with foil. Remove the seafood from the marinade, reserving the remaining marinade, and thread an equal quantity onto each prepared skewer, leaving a little space between each piece. Arrange in the broiler pan.

Cook the skewers under the broiler, turning once and brushing with the reserved marinade, for 6–8 minutes, or until cooked through. Serve hot, drizzled with the marinade in the broiler pan and with lime wedges for squeezing over.

batter-fried fish sticks

To make the batter, put the flour and salt into a large bowl and make a well in the center. Pour the egg and olive oil into the well, then gradually add the water, mixing in the flour from the side and beating constantly, until all the flour is incorporated and a smooth batter forms.

Cut the fish into sticks about 3/4 inch/2 cm wide and 2 inches/5 cm long. Dust lightly with flour so that the batter sticks to them when dipped in it.

Heat enough sunflower or olive oil for deep-frying in a deep-fat fryer to 350–375°F/180–190°C, or until a cube of bread browns in 30 seconds. Spear a fish stick onto a toothpick and dip into the batter, then drop the fish and toothpick into the hot oil. Cook the fish sticks, in batches to avoid overcrowding, for 5 minutes, or until golden brown. Remove with a slotted spoon or draining basket and drain on paper towels. Keep hot in a warm oven while cooking the remaining fish sticks.

Serve the fish sticks hot, with lemon wedges for squeezing over.

SERVES 6
as part of a tapas meal

heaping 3/4 cup all-purpose
    flour, plus extra for dusting
pinch of salt
1 egg, beaten
1 tbsp Spanish olive oil
2/3 cup water
1 lb 5 oz/600 g firm-fleshed
    whitefish fillet, such as
    monkfish or hake
sunflower or Spanish olive oil,
    for deep-frying
lemon wedges, for serving

tuna-stuffed bell pepper strips

SERVES 8
as part of a tapas meal

6 mixed red, green, yellow,
  or orange bell peppers
2 tbsp Spanish olive oil
7 oz/200 g canned tuna in olive
  oil, drained
scant 1/2 cup curd cheese
4 tbsp chopped fresh flat-leaf
  parsley
1 garlic clove, crushed
salt and pepper

Preheat the oven to 400°F/200°C. Brush the bell peppers with the oil and put in a roasting pan. Roast in the preheated oven for 30 minutes, then turn over and roast for an additional 10 minutes, or until the skins have blistered and blackened.

Using a slotted spoon, transfer the roasted peppers to a plastic bag and let cool for about 15 minutes, or until cool enough to handle.

Meanwhile, put the tuna on paper towels and pat dry to remove the oil. Transfer to a food processor, then add the curd cheese, parsley, and garlic and process until mixed together. Season to taste with salt and pepper. Using a sharp knife or your fingers, carefully peel away the skins from the cooled bell peppers. Cut the bell peppers into quarters and remove the stems, cores, and seeds.

Put a heaping teaspoonful of the tuna and cheese mixture on the pointed end of each bell pepper quarter and roll up. If necessary, wipe with paper towels to remove any filling that has spread over the skins, then arrange the rolls in a shallow dish with the filling end facing up. Cover and chill in the refrigerator for at least 2 hours, until firm, before serving.

empanadillas with tuna & olives

SERVES 16
as part of a tapas meal

6 oz/175 g canned tuna in
    olive oil
1 small onion, finely chopped
1 garlic clove, finely chopped
1³/₄ oz/50 g pimiento-stuffed
    Spanish olives, finely chopped
heaping ¹/₈ cup pine nuts
salt and pepper
1 lb 2 oz/500 g prepared puff
    pastry, thawed if frozen
all-purpose flour, for dusting
beaten egg, for glazing

Drain the tuna, reserving the oil, put in a large bowl, and set aside. Heat
1 tablespoon of the reserved oil from the tuna in a large skillet, then add
the onion and cook over medium heat, stirring occasionally, for 5 minutes,
or until softened but not browned. Add the garlic and cook, stirring, for
30 seconds, or until softened.

Mash the tuna with a fork, then add the onion mixture, olives, and pine
nuts and mix together well. Season to taste with salt and pepper.

Preheat the oven to 400°F/200°C. Dampen several large cookie sheets.
Thinly roll out the pastry on a lightly floured counter. Using a plain,
3¹/₄-inch/8-cm round cutter, cut out 32 circles, rerolling the trimmings
as necessary. Using a teaspoon, put an equal, small amount of the tuna
mixture in the center of each pastry circle. Dampen the edges of the
pastry with a little water and fold one half over the other to form a
crescent and enclose the filling. Pinch the edges together with your fingers
to seal, then press with the tines of a fork to seal further. Transfer to the
prepared cookie sheets.

With the tip of a sharp knife, make a small slit in the top of each pastry
and brush with beaten egg to glaze. Bake in the preheated oven for
15 minutes, or until risen and golden brown. Serve warm.

seared squid & golden potatoes

Put the potatoes in a pan of water and bring to a boil. Reduce the heat and simmer for 20 minutes, or until tender. Drain well.

Heat 4 tablespoons of oil in a large ovenproof casserole, then add the potatoes and cook over medium heat, stirring occasionally, for 10 minutes, or until beginning to turn brown. Add the onion and cook, stirring occasionally, for 10 minutes, or until golden brown. Add the garlic and cook, stirring, for 30 seconds until softened. Push all the ingredients to the side of the casserole.

If necessary, add the remaining oil to the casserole. Add the squid slices and cook over high heat, stirring occasionally, for 2 minutes, or until golden brown. Add the wine and cook for an additional 1–2 minutes. Add most of the parsley, reserving a little to garnish, and mix the potatoes, onions, and garlic with the squid. Season to taste with salt and pepper.

Serve hot, in the casserole, sprinkled with the reserved parsley for garnish and with lemon wedges for squeezing over.

SERVES 8
as part of a tapas meal

2 lb 4 oz/1 kg new potatoes
4–6 tbsp Spanish olive oil
1 large onion, thinly sliced
2 garlic cloves, finely chopped
2 lb 4 oz/1 kg cleaned squid
    bodies, thinly sliced
6 tbsp dry white wine
1 small bunch of fresh flat-leaf
    parsley, finely chopped
salt and pepper
lemon wedges, for serving

calamari with shrimp & fava beans

SERVES 4–6
as part of a tapas meal

2 tbsp Spanish olive oil
4 scallions, thinly sliced
2 garlic cloves, finely chopped
1 lb 2 oz/500 g cleaned squid
   bodies, thickly sliced
1/3 cup dry white wine
1 lb 5 oz/600 g fresh young fava
   beans in their pods, shelled
   to give about 8 oz/225 g, or
   8 oz/225 g frozen baby fava
   beans
9 oz/250 g raw jumbo shrimp,
   shelled and deveined
4 tbsp chopped fresh flat-leaf
   parsley
salt and pepper
crusty bread, for serving

Heat the oil in a large skillet with a lid or an ovenproof casserole. Add the scallions and cook over medium heat, stirring occasionally, for 4–5 minutes, or until softened. Add the garlic and cook, stirring, for 30 seconds, or until softened. Add the squid slices and cook over high heat, stirring occasionally, for 2 minutes, or until golden brown.

Add the wine and bring to a boil. Add the fava beans and reduce the heat, then cover and simmer, for 5–8 minutes if using fresh beans or 4–5 minutes if using frozen beans, until the beans are tender.

Add the shrimp and parsley, re-cover, and simmer for an additional 2–3 minutes, or until the shrimp turn pink and start to curl. Season to taste with salt and pepper. Serve hot, with crusty bread to mop up the juices.

tossed shrimp with bell peppers

SERVES 8
as part of a tapas meal

1 lb 2 oz/500 g raw jumbo
  shrimp, in their shells
2 tbsp Spanish olive oil
2 red bell peppers, cored,
  seeded, and thinly sliced
5 garlic cloves, finely chopped
juice of ½ lemon
6 tbsp dry Spanish sherry
salt and pepper
crusty bread, for serving

Pull off the heads of the shrimp. With your fingers, peel away the shells, leaving the tails intact. Using a sharp knife, make a shallow slit along the length of the back of each shrimp, then use the tip of the knife to lift out the dark vein and discard. Rinse the shrimp under cold running water and pat dry with paper towels.

Heat the oil in a large skillet, then add the red bell pepper slices and cook for 10–15 minutes, or until softened. Add the garlic and cook, stirring, for 30 seconds until softened. Add the shrimp to the skillet and cook, tossing constantly, for 1–2 minutes, or until the shrimp turn pink. Add the lemon juice and sherry and cook for an additional 2 minutes, or until the shrimp begin to curl. Season to taste with salt and pepper.

Serve hot, with chunks or slices of crusty bread to mop up the juices.

sizzling chile shrimp

Pull the heads off the shrimp and peel, leaving the tails intact. Cut along the length of the back of each shrimp and remove and discard the dark vein. Rinse the shrimp under cold running water and pat dry on paper towels.

Cut the chile in half lengthwise, then remove the seeds and finely chop the flesh.

Heat the oil in a large, heavy-bottom skillet or flameproof casserole until quite hot, then add the garlic and cook for 30 seconds. Add the shrimp, chile, paprika, and a pinch of salt and cook for 2–3 minutes, stirring constantly, until the shrimp turn pink and begin to curl.

Serve the shrimp in the cooking dish, still sizzling. Accompany with wooden toothpicks, to spear the shrimp, and chunks or slices of crusty bread to mop up the aromatic cooking oil.

SERVES 6
as part of a tapas meal

1 lb 2 oz/500 g raw jumbo
   shrimp, in their shells
1 small fresh red chile
6 tbsp Spanish olive oil
2 garlic cloves, finely chopped
pinch of paprika
salt
crusty bread, for serving

saffron shrimp with lemon mayonnaise

SERVES 6–8
as part of a tapas meal

2 lb 12 oz/1.25 kg raw
   jumbo shrimp
heaping 1/2 cup all-purpose
   flour
1/2 cup light beer
2 tbsp Spanish olive oil
pinch of saffron powder
2 egg whites
vegetable oil, for deep-frying

for the lemon mayonnaise
4 garlic cloves
2 egg yolks
1 tbsp lemon juice
1 tbsp finely grated lemon rind
1 1/4 cups corn oil
sea salt and pepper

First make the mayonnaise. Place the garlic cloves on a cutting board and sprinkle with a little sea salt, then flatten them with the side of a heavy knife. Finely chop and flatten again.

Transfer the garlic to a food processor or blender and add the egg yolks, lemon juice, and lemon rind. Process briefly until just blended. With the motor still running, gradually add the corn oil through the feeder tube until it is fully incorporated. Scrape the mayonnaise into a serving bowl and season to taste with salt and pepper, then cover and let chill until ready to serve.

Pull the heads off the shrimp and peel, leaving the tails intact. Cut along the length of the back of each shrimp and remove and discard the dark vein. Rinse under cold running water and pat dry with paper towels.

Sift the flour into a bowl. Mix the beer, oil, and saffron together in a pitcher, then gradually whisk into the flour. Cover and let stand at room temperature for 30 minutes to rest.

Whisk the egg whites in a spotlessly clean, greasefree bowl until stiff. Gently fold the egg whites into the flour mixture.

Heat the vegetable oil in a deep-fat fryer or large pan to 350–375°F/ 180–190°C, or until a cube of bread browns in 30 seconds. Holding the shrimp by their tails, dip them into the batter and shake off any excess. Add the shrimp to the oil and deep-fry for 2–3 minutes, or until crisp. Remove with a slotted spoon and drain well on paper towels. Serve immediately with the mayonnaise.

crab tartlets

SERVES 12
as part of a tapas meal

1 tbsp Spanish olive oil
1 small onion, finely chopped
1 garlic clove, finely chopped
splash of dry white wine
2 eggs
2/3 cup milk or light cream
6 oz/175 g canned crabmeat,
    drained
2 oz/55 g Manchego or
    Parmesan cheese, grated
2 tbsp chopped fresh flat-leaf
    parsley
pinch of freshly grated nutmeg
salt and pepper
fresh dill sprigs, for garnish

for the pastry
2 1/3 cups all-purpose flour,
    plus extra for dusting
pinch of salt
3/4 cup butter
2 tbsp cold water

or
1 lb 2 oz/500 g prepared
    unsweetened pie pastry

Preheat the oven to 375°F/190°C. To prepare the crabmeat filling, heat the olive oil in a pan. Add the onion and cook for 5 minutes, or until softened but not browned. Add the garlic and cook for an additional 30 seconds. Add a splash of white wine and cook for 1–2 minutes, or until most of the wine has evaporated.

Lightly whisk the eggs in a large bowl, then whisk in the milk or cream. Add the crabmeat, grated cheese, parsley, and the onion mixture. Season the mixture with nutmeg and salt and pepper to taste and mix together.

To prepare the pastry if you are making it yourself, mix the flour and salt together in a large bowl. Add the butter, cut into small pieces, and rub it in until the mixture resembles fine breadcrumbs. Gradually stir in enough of the water to form a firm dough. Alternatively, the pastry could be made in a food processor.

Thinly roll out the pastry on a lightly floured counter. Using a plain, round 2 3/4-inch/7-cm cutter, cut the pastry into 18 circles. Gently pile the trimmings together and roll out again, then cut out an additional 6 circles. Use to line 24 x 1 1/2-inch/4-cm tartlet pans. Carefully spoon the crabmeat mixture into the pastry shells, taking care not to overfill them.

Bake the tartlets in the preheated oven for 25–30 minutes, or until golden brown and set. Serve the crab tartlets hot or cold, garnished with fresh dill sprigs.

sweet peppers stuffed with crab salad

First make the crab salad. Pick over the crabmeat and remove any bits of shell. Put half the crabmeat in a food processor with the prepared red bell pepper, 1 1/2 tablespoons of the lemon juice, and salt and pepper to taste. Process until well blended, then transfer to a bowl. Stir in the cream cheese and remaining crabmeat. Taste and add extra lemon juice, if needed.

Pat the pimientos del piquillo dry and scoop out any seeds that remain in the tips. Use a small spoon to divide the crab salad equally among the pimientos, stuffing them generously. Arrange on a large serving dish or individual plates, then cover and let chill until ready to serve. Just before serving, sprinkle the stuffed pimientos with the chopped parsley.

SERVES 8
as part of a tapas meal

16 pimientos del piquillo,
    drained, or freshly roasted
    sweet peppers, tops cut off
chopped fresh parsley,
    for garnish

for the crab salad
8 1/2 oz/240 g canned crabmeat,
    drained and squeezed dry
1 red bell pepper, roasted,
    peeled, and chopped
about 2 tbsp fresh lemon juice
salt and pepper
scant 1 cup cream cheese

scallops with serrano ham

SERVES 4
as part of a tapas meal

2 tbsp lemon juice
3 tbsp Spanish olive oil
2 garlic cloves, finely chopped
1 tbsp chopped fresh parsley
12 shelled scallops, preferably
  with corals
8 wafer-thin slices Serrano ham
pepper

Mix the lemon juice, olive oil, garlic, and parsley together in a nonmetallic dish. Separate the corals, if using, from the scallops and add both to the dish, turning to coat. Cover with plastic wrap and let marinate at room temperature for 20 minutes.

Preheat the broiler to medium. Drain the scallops, reserving the marinade. Thread a scallop and a coral, if using, onto a metal skewer. Scrunch up a slice of ham and thread onto the skewer, followed by another scallop and a coral. Repeat to fill 4 skewers, each with 3 scallops and 2 slices of ham.

Cook under the hot broiler, basting with the marinade and turning frequently, for 5 minutes, or until the scallops are tender and the ham is crisp.

Transfer to warmed serving plates and sprinkle them with pepper. Spoon over the cooking juices from the broiler pan and serve.

mussels in a vinaigrette dressing

SERVES 6
as part of a tapas meal

6 tbsp Spanish extra virgin
 olive oil
2 tbsp white wine vinegar
1 shallot, finely chopped
1 garlic clove, crushed
2 tbsp capers, chopped
1 fresh red chile, seeded and
 finely chopped (optional)
salt and pepper
2 lb 4 oz/1 kg live mussels,
 in their shells
6 tbsp dry white wine
4 tbsp chopped fresh flat-leaf
 parsley
crusty bread, for serving
 (optional)

To make the dressing, put the oil and vinegar in a bowl and whisk together. Stir in the shallot, garlic, capers, and chile, if using. Season to taste with salt and pepper.

Clean the mussels by scrubbing or scraping the shells and pulling out any beards that are attached to them. Discard any with broken shells or any that refuse to close when tapped. Put the mussels in a colander and rinse well under cold running water.

Put the mussels in a large pan and add the wine. Bring to a boil, then cover and cook over high heat, shaking the pan occasionally, for 3–4 minutes, or until the mussels have opened. Drain the mussels, discarding any that remain closed, and let cool.

When the mussels are cool enough to handle, discard the empty half-shells and arrange the mussels, in their other half-shells, in a large, shallow serving dish. Discard any mussels that remain closed. Whisk the dressing again and spoon over the mussels. Cover and chill in the refrigerator for at least 1 hour.

To serve, sprinkle the parsley over the top and serve with crusty bread, if using, to mop up the dressing.

mussels with garlic butter

Clean the mussels by scrubbing or scraping the shells and pulling out any beards that are attached to them. Discard any with broken shells and any that refuse to close when sharply tapped with the back of a knife. Place the mussels in a colander and rinse under cold running water.

Place the mussels in a large pan and add a splash of wine and the bay leaf. Cook, covered, over high heat for 5 minutes, shaking the pan occasionally, or until the mussels are opened. Drain the mussels and discard any that remain closed.

Shell the mussels, reserving one half of each shell. Arrange the mussels, in their half-shells, in a large, shallow, ovenproof serving dish.

Melt the butter and pour into a bowl. Add the breadcrumbs, parsley, chives, and garlic and season to taste with salt and pepper, then mix well together. Let stand until the butter has set slightly. Using your fingers or 2 teaspoons, take a large pinch of the herb and butter mixture and use to fill each mussel shell, pressing it down well. Let the mussels chill until ready to serve.

To serve, preheat the oven to 450°F/230°C. Bake the mussels in the preheated oven for 10 minutes, or until hot. Serve immediately, garnished with parsley sprigs and accompanied by lemon wedges for squeezing over them.

SERVES 8
as part of a tapas meal

1 lb 12 oz/800 g live mussels, in their shells
splash of dry white wine
1 bay leaf
1/2 cup butter
12 oz/350 g fresh white or whole wheat breadcrumbs
4 tbsp chopped fresh flat-leaf parsley, plus extra sprigs for garnish
2 tbsp snipped fresh chives
2 garlic cloves, finely chopped
salt and pepper
lemon wedges, for serving

oysters with sherry vinegar

SERVES 6
as part of a tapas meal

1 shallot, finely chopped
3 tbsp sherry vinegar
3 tbsp red wine vinegar
1 tbsp sugar
pepper
24 fresh oysters
rock salt or crushed ice,
    for serving (optional)

Mix the shallot, vinegars, and sugar together in a nonmetallic bowl and season well with pepper. Cover with plastic wrap and let stand at room temperature for at least 15 minutes so that the flavors mingle.

Meanwhile, shuck the oysters. Wrap a dish towel around your hand to protect it and hold an oyster firmly. Insert an oyster knife or other strong, sharp knife into the hinged edge and twist to pry the shells apart. Still holding both shells firmly in the wrapped hand, slide the blade of the knife along the upper shell to sever the muscle. Lift off the upper shell, being careful not to spill the liquid inside. Slide the blade of the knife along the lower shell underneath the oyster to sever the second muscle. Arrange the oysters on their half shells in a single layer on a bed of rock salt or crushed ice, if you like.

Spoon the dressing evenly over the oysters and serve at room temperature.

clams in tomato & garlic sauce

SERVES 6–8
as part of a tapas meal

2 hard-cooked eggs, cooled,
    shelled, and halved lengthwise
3 tbsp Spanish olive oil
1 Spanish onion, chopped
2 garlic cloves, finely chopped
1 lb 9 oz/700 g tomatoes,
    peeled and diced
3/4 cup fresh white
    breadcrumbs
salt and pepper
2 lb 4 oz/1 kg fresh clams
1 3/4 cups dry white wine
2 tbsp chopped fresh parsley
lemon wedges, for garnish

Scoop out the egg yolks using a teaspoon and rub through a fine strainer into a bowl. Chop the whites and reserve separately.

Heat the olive oil in a large, heavy-bottom skillet. Add the onion and cook over low heat, stirring occasionally, for 5 minutes, or until softened. Add the garlic and cook for an additional 3 minutes, then add the tomatoes, breadcrumbs, and egg yolks and season to taste with salt and pepper. Cook, stirring occasionally and mashing the mixture with a wooden spoon, for an additional 10–15 minutes, or until thick and pulpy.

Meanwhile, scrub the clams under cold running water. Discard any with broken shells or any that do not close immediately when sharply tapped with the back of a knife.

Place the clams in a large, heavy-bottom pan. Add the wine and bring to a boil. Cover and cook over high heat, shaking the pan occasionally, for 3–5 minutes, or until the clams have opened. Discard any that remain closed.

Using a slotted spoon, transfer the clams to warmed serving bowls. Strain the cooking liquid into the tomato sauce, then stir well and spoon over the clams. Sprinkle with the chopped egg whites and parsley and serve immediately, garnished with lemon wedges.

eggs & cheese

Eggs and cheese are two essential ingredients in Spanish cooking, offering great scope for many inexpensive tapas recipes. Nothing symbolizes the essence of tapas more than the thick egg and potato omelet called Spanish Tortilla. Made with such humble ingredients, once a meager meal for poor laborers, it is now the nation's favorite tapas. This chapter also contains many satisfying variations, but whichever you try, it will be delicious hot or at room temperature. Oven-baked Tortilla, cut into tiny squares and speared on toothpicks, makes a good party dish. Cheese Puffs with Fiery Tomato Salsa are perennially popular, while Figs with Bleu Cheese make good use of wonderfully fresh ingredients.

spanish tortilla

SERVES 8
as part of a tapas meal

1/2 cup Spanish olive oil
1 lb 5 oz/600 g potatoes, peeled
   and thinly sliced
1 large onion, thinly sliced
6 large eggs
salt and pepper
fresh flat-leaf parsley,
   for garnish

Heat a nonstick 10-inch/25-cm skillet over high heat. Add the olive oil and heat. Reduce the heat, then add the potatoes and onion and cook for 15–20 minutes, or until the potatoes are tender.

Beat the eggs in a large bowl and season generously with salt and pepper. Drain the potatoes and onion through a strainer over a heatproof bowl to reserve the oil. Very gently stir the vegetables into the eggs, then let stand for 10 minutes.

Use a wooden spoon or spatula to remove any crusty bits stuck to the base of the skillet. Reheat the skillet over medium heat with 4 tablespoons of the reserved oil.

Add the egg mixture and smooth the surface, pressing the potatoes and onions into an even layer.

Cook for 5 minutes, shaking the skillet occasionally, until the base is set. Use a spatula to loosen the side of the tortilla. Place a large plate over the top and carefully invert the skillet and plate together so the tortilla drops onto the plate.

Add 1 tablespoon of the remaining reserved oil to the skillet and swirl around. Carefully slide the tortilla back into the skillet, cooked-side up. Run the spatula around the tortilla, to tuck in the edge.

Continue cooking for 3 minutes, or until the eggs are set and the base is golden brown. Remove the skillet from the heat and slide the tortilla onto a plate. Let stand for at least 5 minutes before cutting. Garnish with parsley and serve.

oven–baked tortilla

SERVES 16
as part of a tapas meal

4 tbsp Spanish olive oil, plus
    extra for oiling
1 large garlic clove, crushed
4 scallions, white and green
    parts finely chopped
1 green bell pepper, seeded
    and finely diced
1 red bell pepper, seeded and
    finely diced
6 oz/175 g potato, boiled,
    peeled, and diced
5 large eggs
scant 1/2 cup sour cream
6 oz/175 g Spanish Rocal,
    Cheddar, or Parmesan
    cheese, grated
3 tbsp snipped fresh chives
salt and pepper
slices of bread, for serving
green salad, for serving

Preheat the oven to 375°F/190°C. Line a 7 x 10-inch/18 x 25-cm baking sheet with foil and brush with a little olive oil. Reserve.

Place the olive oil, garlic, scallions, and bell peppers in a skillet and cook over medium heat, stirring, for 10 minutes, or until the onions are softened but not browned. Let cool, then stir in the potato.

Beat the eggs, sour cream, cheese, and chives together in a large bowl. Stir the cooled vegetables into the bowl and season to taste with salt and pepper.

Pour the mixture into the baking sheet and smooth over the top. Bake in the preheated oven for 30–40 minutes, or until golden brown, puffed, and set in the center. Remove from the oven and let cool and set. Run a spatula around the edge, then invert onto a cutting board, browned-side up, and peel off the foil. If the surface looks a little runny, place it under a medium broiler to dry out.

Let cool completely. Trim the edges if necessary, then cut into 48 squares. Serve on a platter with wooden toothpicks, or secure each square to a slice of bread, and accompany with a green salad.

chorizo & fava bean tortilla

Cook the fava beans in a pan of boiling water for 4 minutes. Drain well and let cool. Meanwhile, lightly beat the eggs in a large bowl. Add the chorizo sausage and season to taste with salt and pepper.

When the beans are cool enough to handle, slip off their skins. This is a laborious task, but worth doing if you have the time. This quantity will take about 15 minutes to skin.

Heat the oil in a large skillet, then add the onion and cook over medium heat, stirring occasionally, for 5 minutes, or until softened but not browned. Add the fava beans and cook, stirring, for 1 minute. Pour the egg mixture into the skillet and cook gently for 2–3 minutes, or until the underside is just set and lightly browned. Use a spatula to loosen the tortilla away from the side and bottom of the skillet to let the uncooked egg run underneath and prevent the tortilla from sticking to the bottom.

Cover the tortilla with a large, upside-down plate and invert the tortilla onto it. Slide the tortilla back into the skillet, cooked-side up, and cook for an additional 2–3 minutes, or until the underside is lightly browned.

Slide the tortilla onto a warmed serving dish. Serve warm, cut into small cubes.

SERVES 8
as part of a tapas meal

8 oz/225 g frozen baby
  fava beans
6 eggs
3 1/2 oz/100 g chorizo sausage,
  outer casing removed,
  chopped
salt and pepper
3 tbsp Spanish olive oil
1 onion, chopped

spinach & mushroom tortilla

SERVES 8
as part of a tapas meal

2 tbsp Spanish olive oil
3 shallots, finely chopped
12 oz/350 g mushrooms, sliced
10 oz/280 g fresh spinach
    leaves, coarse stems
    removed
salt and pepper
2 oz/55 g toasted slivered
    almonds
5 eggs
2 tbsp chopped fresh parsley
2 tbsp cold water
3 oz/85 g mature Mahon,
    Manchego, or Parmesan
    cheese, grated

Heat the olive oil in a skillet that can safely be placed under the broiler. Add the shallots and cook over low heat, stirring occasionally, for 5 minutes, or until softened. Add the mushrooms and cook, stirring frequently, for an additional 4 minutes. Add the spinach, then increase the heat to medium and cook, stirring frequently, for 3–4 minutes, or until wilted. Reduce the heat, then season to taste with salt and pepper and stir in the slivered almonds.

Beat the eggs with the parsley, water, and salt and pepper to taste in a bowl. Pour the mixture into the skillet and cook for 5–8 minutes, or until the underside is set. Lift the edge of the tortilla occasionally to let the uncooked egg run underneath. Meanwhile, preheat the broiler to high.

Sprinkle the grated cheese over the tortilla and cook under the preheated hot broiler for 3 minutes, or until the top is set and the cheese has melted. Serve, lukewarm or cold, cut into thin wedges.

eggplant tortilla wedges

SERVES 8–10
as part of a tapas meal

1 lb 2 oz/500 g eggplants
1/2 cup Spanish olive oil
1 onion, chopped
6 eggs
salt and pepper
chopped fresh flat-leaf parsley,
    for garnish (optional)

Cut the eggplants into 1/4-inch/5-mm thick slices. Heat 2 tablespoons of the oil in a large skillet, then add the onion and cook over medium heat, stirring occasionally, for 5 minutes, or until softened but not browned. Add the remaining oil to the skillet and heat until hot. Add the eggplant slices and cook over medium heat, turning occasionally, for 15–20 minutes until tender.

Meanwhile, lightly beat the eggs in a large bowl and season generously with salt and pepper. When the eggplants are cooked, drain in a strainer set over a large bowl to catch the oil. When well drained, gently stir into the beaten eggs. Wipe the skillet clean or wash, if necessary, to prevent the tortilla from sticking. Pour the reserved oil into the skillet and heat. Add the egg and eggplant mixture and cook gently for 3–4 minutes, or until the underside is just set and lightly browned. Use a spatula to loosen the tortilla away from the side and bottom of the skillet to let most of the uncooked egg run underneath and prevent the tortilla from sticking to the bottom.

Cover the tortilla with a large, upside-down plate and invert the tortilla onto it. Slide the tortilla back into the skillet, cooked-side up, and cook for an additional 3–4 minutes, or until the underside is lightly browned.

Slide the tortilla onto a warmed serving dish. Cut the tortilla into wedges and serve warm, sprinkled generously with chopped parsley, if using.

deviled eggs

To cook the eggs, place them in a pan, then cover with cold water and slowly bring to a boil. Immediately reduce the heat to very low, then cover and simmer gently for 10 minutes. As soon as the eggs are cooked, drain and place under cold running water until they are cold. By doing this quickly, it will prevent a black ring from forming around the egg yolk. Gently tap the eggs to crack the eggshells and let stand until cold. When cold, crack the shells and remove them.

Using a stainless steel knife, halve the eggs lengthwise, then carefully remove the yolks. Place the yolks in a nylon strainer set over a bowl and rub through, then mash them with a wooden spoon or fork. If necessary, rinse the egg whites under cold running water and dry carefully.

Place the pimientos on paper towels to dry well, then chop them finely, reserving a few strips. Finely chop half of the olives. Halve the remaining olives and reserve. If you are going to pipe the filling into the eggs, you need to chop both these ingredients very finely so that they will go through a 1/2-inch/1-cm nozzle. Add the chopped pimientos and chopped olives to the mashed egg yolks. Add the mayonnaise, mix together well, then add the Tabasco, cayenne, and salt and pepper to taste.

For a grand finale, place the egg yolk mixture into a pastry bag fitted with a 1/2-inch/1-cm plain tip and pipe the mixture into the hollow egg whites. Alternatively, for a simpler finish, use a teaspoon to spoon the prepared filling into each egg half.

Arrange the eggs on a serving plate. Add 1–2 small strips of the reserved pimientos and an olive half to the top of each stuffed egg. Dust with a little paprika and garnish with lettuce leaves, then serve.

SERVES 8
as part of a tapas meal

8 large eggs
2 whole canned or bottled
  pimientos del piquillo
16 pitted green Spanish olives
5 tbsp mayonnaise
8 drops of Tabasco sauce
large pinch of cayenne pepper
salt and pepper
paprika, for dusting
lettuce leaves, for garnish

stuffed eggs with anchovies & cheese

SERVES 8
as part of a tapas meal

8 eggs
1³/₄ oz/50 g canned anchovy
   fillets in olive oil, drained
2 oz/55 g Manchego cheese,
   grated
4 tbsp Spanish extra virgin
   olive oil
1 tbsp freshly squeezed lemon
   juice
1 garlic clove, crushed
salt and pepper
4 pitted black Spanish olives,
   halved
4 pitted green Spanish olives,
   halved
hot or sweet smoked Spanish
   paprika, for dusting

Put the eggs in a pan, then cover with cold water and slowly bring to a boil. Reduce the heat and simmer gently for 10 minutes. Immediately drain the eggs and rinse under cold running water to cool. Gently tap the eggs to crack the shells and let stand until cold.

When the eggs are cold, crack the shells all over and remove them. Using a stainless steel knife, halve the eggs, then carefully remove the egg yolks and put in a food processor.

Add the anchovy fillets, Manchego cheese, oil, lemon juice, and garlic to the egg yolks and process to a purée. Season to taste with salt and pepper.

Using a teaspoon, spoon the mixture into the egg white halves. Alternatively, using a pastry bag fitted with a ¹/₂-inch/1-cm plain tip, pipe the mixture into the egg white halves. Arrange the eggs in a serving dish, then cover and chill in the refrigerator until ready to serve.

For serving, put an olive half on the top of each stuffed egg and dust with paprika.

eggs & cheese

SERVES 6
as part of a tapas meal

6 hard-cooked eggs, cooled and
   shelled
3 tbsp grated Manchego or
   Cheddar cheese
1–2 tbsp mayonnaise
2 tbsp snipped fresh chives
1 fresh red chile, seeded and
   finely chopped
salt and pepper
lettuce leaves, for serving

Cut the eggs in half lengthwise and, using a teaspoon, carefully scoop out the yolks into a fine strainer, reserving the egg white halves. Rub the yolks through the strainer into a bowl and add the grated cheese, mayonnaise, chives, chile, and salt and pepper to taste.

Spoon the filling into the egg white halves.

Arrange a bed of lettuce on individual serving plates and top with the eggs. Cover and let chill until ready to serve.

asparagus & fried eggs

Trim and discard the coarse, woody ends of the asparagus spears. Make sure all the stems are about the same length, then tie them together loosely with clean kitchen string. If you have an asparagus steamer, you don't need to tie the stems together—just place them in the basket.

Bring a tall pan of lightly salted water to a boil. Add the asparagus, making sure that the tips are protruding above the water, then reduce the heat and let simmer for 10–15 minutes, or until tender. Test by piercing a stem just above the water level with the point of a sharp knife.

Meanwhile, heat a little of the olive oil in a large, heavy-bottom skillet. Add 2 eggs, if there is enough room, and cook over medium-low heat, or until the whites are just set and the yolks are still runny. Transfer to warmed serving plates and cook the remaining eggs in the same way.

Drain the asparagus and divide the spears among the plates. Serve immediately.

SERVES 6
as part of a tapas meal

1 lb 2 oz/500 g asparagus
   spears
2 tbsp Spanish olive oil
6 eggs

asparagus scrambled eggs

SERVES 6
as part of a tapas meal

1 lb/450 g asparagus, trimmed
  and coarsely chopped
2 tbsp Spanish olive oil
1 onion, finely chopped
1 garlic clove, finely chopped
6 eggs
1 tbsp water
salt and pepper
6 small slices country bread

Steam the asparagus pieces for 8 minutes or cook in a large pan of boiling salted water for 4 minutes, or until just tender, depending on their thickness. Drain well, if necessary.

Meanwhile, heat the oil in a large skillet, then add the onion and cook over medium heat, stirring occasionally, for 5 minutes, or until softened but not browned. Add the garlic and cook, stirring, for 30 seconds until softened.

Stir the asparagus into the skillet and cook, stirring occasionally, for 3–4 minutes. Meanwhile, break the eggs into a bowl, then add the water and beat together. Season to taste with salt and pepper.

Preheat the broiler to high. Add the beaten eggs to the asparagus mixture and cook, stirring constantly, for 2 minutes, or until the eggs have just set. Remove from the heat.

Toast the bread slices under the broiler until golden brown on both sides. Pile the scrambled eggs on top of the toast and serve immediately.

basque scrambled eggs

SERVES 4–6
as part of a tapas meal

2–4 tbsp Spanish olive oil
1 large onion, chopped finely
1 large red bell pepper, cored,
    seeded, and chopped
1 large green bell pepper,
    cored, seeded, and chopped
2 large tomatoes, peeled,
    seeded, and chopped
2 oz/55 g chorizo sausage,
    sliced thinly, casings
    removed, if preferred
3 tbsp butter
10 large eggs, beaten lightly
salt and pepper
4–6 thick slices country-style
    bread, toasted, for serving

Heat 2 tablespoons of the oil in a large, heavy-bottom skillet over medium-high heat. Add the onion and bell peppers and cook for about 5 minutes, or until the vegetables are soft, but not brown. Add the tomatoes and heat through. Transfer to a plate and keep warm in a preheated low oven.

Add another tablespoon of oil to the skillet. Add the chorizo and cook for 30 seconds, just to warm through and flavor the oil. Add the sausage to the reserved vegetables.

There should be about 2 tablespoons of oil in the skillet, so add a little extra, if necessary, to make up the amount. Add the butter and let melt. Season the eggs with salt and pepper, then add them to the skillet. Scramble the eggs until they are cooked to the desired degree of firmness. Add extra seasoning to taste. Return the vegetables to the skillet and stir through. Serve immediately with hot toast.

flamenco eggs

Preheat the oven to 350°F/180°C. Heat the olive oil in a large, heavy-bottom skillet. Add the onion and garlic and cook over low heat, stirring occasionally, for 5 minutes, or until softened. Add the red bell peppers and cook, stirring occasionally, for an additional 10 minutes. Stir in the tomatoes and parsley, season to taste with salt and cayenne and cook for an additional 5 minutes. Stir in the corn kernels and remove the skillet from the heat.

Divide the mixture among 4 individual ovenproof dishes. Make a hollow in the surface of each using the back of a spoon. Break an egg into each depression.

Bake in the preheated oven for 15–25 minutes, or until the eggs have set. Serve hot.

SERVES 4
as part of a tapas meal

4 tbsp Spanish olive oil
1 onion, thinly sliced
2 garlic cloves, finely chopped
2 small red bell peppers,
   seeded and chopped
4 tomatoes, peeled, seeded,
   and chopped
1 tbsp chopped fresh parsley
salt and cayenne pepper
7 oz/200 g canned corn kernels,
   drained
4 eggs

baked tomato nests

SERVES 4
as part of a tapas meal

4 large ripe tomatoes
salt and pepper
4 large eggs
4 tbsp heavy cream
4 tbsp grated aged Mahon,
   Manchego, or Parmesan
   cheese

Preheat the oven to 350°F/180°C. Cut a slice off the tops of the tomatoes and, using a teaspoon, carefully scoop out the pulp and seeds without piercing the shells. Turn the tomato shells upside down on paper towels and let drain for 15 minutes. Season the insides of the shells with salt and pepper.

Place the tomatoes in an ovenproof dish just large enough to hold them in a single layer. Carefully break 1 egg into each tomato shell, then top with 1 tablespoon of cream and 1 tablespoon of grated cheese.

Bake in the preheated oven for 15–20 minutes, or until the eggs are just set. Serve hot.

cheese puffs with fiery tomato salsa

SERVES 8
as part of a tapas meal

1/2 cup all-purpose flour
1/4 cup Spanish olive oil
2/3 cup water
2 eggs, beaten
2 oz/55 g Manchego, Parmesan,
    Cheddar, Gouda, or Gruyère
    cheese, finely grated
1/2 tsp paprika
salt and pepper
corn oil, for deep-frying

for the fiery tomato salsa
2 tbsp Spanish olive oil
1 small onion, finely chopped
1 garlic clove, crushed
splash of dry white wine
14 oz/400 g canned chopped
    tomatoes
1 tbsp tomato paste
1/4–1/2 tsp chile flakes
dash of Tabasco sauce
pinch of sugar
salt and pepper

To make the salsa, heat the olive oil in a pan. Add the onion and cook for 5 minutes, or until softened but not browned. Add the garlic and cook for an additional 30 seconds. Add the wine and let bubble, then add all the remaining salsa ingredients to the pan and simmer, uncovered, for 10–15 minutes, or until a thick sauce has formed. Spoon into a serving bowl and reserve until ready to serve.

Meanwhile, prepare the cheese puffs. Sift the flour onto a plate or sheet of waxed paper. Place the olive oil and water in a pan and slowly bring to a boil. As soon as the water boils, remove from the heat and quickly add the flour all at once. Using a wooden spoon, beat the mixture until it is smooth and leaves the sides of the pan.

Let the mixture cool for 1–2 minutes. Gradually add the eggs, beating hard after each addition and keeping the mixture stiff. Add the cheese and paprika, then season to taste with salt and pepper and mix well. Store in the refrigerator until you are ready to cook the cheese puffs.

Just before serving the cheese puffs, heat the sunflower oil in a deep-fat fryer to 350–375°F/180–190°C, or until a cube of bread browns in 30 seconds. Drop teaspoonfuls of the prepared mixture, in batches, into the hot oil and deep-fry for 2–3 minutes, turning once, or until golden brown and crispy. They should rise to the surface of the oil and puff up. Drain well on paper towels.

Serve the puffs piping hot, accompanied by the fiery salsa for dipping and wooden toothpicks to spear the puffs.

fried manchego cheese

Slice the cheese into triangular shapes about 2 cm/³/₄ inch thick or alternatively into cubes measuring about the same size. Place the flour in a plastic bag and season to taste with salt and pepper. Break the egg into a shallow dish and beat together with the water. Spread the breadcrumbs onto a large plate.

Toss the cheese pieces in the flour so that they are evenly coated, then dip the cheese in the egg mixture. Finally, dip the cheese in the breadcrumbs so that the pieces are coated on all sides. Transfer to a large plate and store in the refrigerator until you are ready to serve them.

Just before serving, heat about 1 inch/2.5 cm of the corn oil in a large, heavy-bottom skillet or deep-fat fryer to 350–375°F/180–190°C, or until a cube of bread browns in 30 seconds. Add the cheese pieces, in batches of about 4 or 5 pieces so that the temperature of the oil does not drop, and deep-fry for 1–2 minutes, turning once, until the cheese is just beginning to melt and they are golden brown on all sides. Do make sure that the oil is hot enough, otherwise the coating on the cheese will take too long to become crisp and the cheese inside may ooze out.

Using a slotted spoon, remove the fried cheese from the skillet or deep-fat fryer and drain well on paper towels. Serve the fried cheese pieces hot, accompanied by wooden toothpicks on which to spear them.

SERVES 6–8
as part of a tapas meal

7 oz/200 g Manchego cheese
3 tbsp all-purpose flour
salt and pepper
1 egg
1 tsp water
1¹/₂ cups fresh white or whole
    wheat breadcrumbs
corn oil, for deep-frying

bell peppers with fiery cheese

SERVES 6
as part of a tapas meal

1 red bell pepper, halved and
  seeded
1 orange bell pepper, halved
  and seeded
1 yellow bell pepper, halved
  and seeded
4 oz/115 g Afuega'l Pitu cheese
  or other hot spiced cheese,
  diced
1 tbsp clear honey
1 tbsp sherry vinegar
salt and pepper

Preheat the broiler to high. Place the bell peppers, skin-side up, in a single layer on a baking sheet. Cook under the hot broiler for 8–10 minutes, or until the skins have blistered and blackened. Using tongs, transfer to a plastic bag. Tie the top and let cool.

When the bell peppers are cool enough to handle, peel off the skin with your fingers or a knife and discard it. Place on a serving plate and sprinkle over the cheese.

Whisk the honey and vinegar together in a bowl and season to taste with salt and pepper. Pour the dressing over the bell peppers, then cover and let chill until ready to serve.

empanadillas with cheese & olives

SERVES 6
as part of a tapas meal

3 oz/85 g firm or soft cheese
1/2 cup pitted green Spanish
   olives
1/3 cup sun-dried tomatoes
   in oil, drained
13/4 oz/50 g canned anchovy
   fillets, drained
pepper
2 oz/55 g sun-dried tomato
   paste
1 lb 2 oz/500 g prepared puff
   pastry, thawed if frozen
all-purpose flour, for dusting
beaten egg, for glazing

Preheat the oven to 400°F/200°C. Cut the cheese into small dice measuring about 1/4 inch/5 mm. Chop the olives, sun-dried tomatoes, and anchovies into pieces about the same size as the cheese. Place all the chopped ingredients in a bowl, then season to taste with pepper and gently mix together. Stir in the sun-dried tomato paste.

Thinly roll out the puff pastry on a lightly floured counter. Using a plain, round 3 1/4-inch/8-cm cutter, cut into 16 circles. Gently pile the trimmings together and roll out again, then cut out an additional 8 circles. Using a teaspoon, place a little of the prepared filling equally in the center of each of the pastry circles.

Dampen the edges of the pastry with a little water, then bring up the sides to completely cover the filling and pinch the edges together with your fingers to seal them. With the point of a sharp knife, make a small slit in the top of each pastry. You can store the pastries in the refrigerator at this stage until you are ready to bake them.

Place the pastries onto dampened baking sheets and brush each with a little beaten egg to glaze. Bake in the preheated oven for 10–15 minutes, or until golden brown, crisp, and well risen. Serve the empanadillas piping hot, warm, or cold.

sun-dried tomato
& goat cheese tarts

Preheat the oven to 425°F/220°C. Dampen a large cookie sheet. Finely chop the sun-dried tomatoes and reserve. Heat 1 tablespoon of the reserved oil from the tomatoes in a large skillet, then add the zucchini slices and cook over medium heat, stirring occasionally, for 8–10 minutes, or until golden brown on both sides. Add the garlic and cook, stirring, for 30 seconds. Remove from the heat and let cool while you prepare the pastry bases.

Thinly roll out the pastry on a lightly floured counter. Using a plain, 3½-inch/9-cm cutter, cut out 1–2 circles, rerolling the trimmings as necessary. Transfer the circles to the prepared cookie sheet and prick 3–4 times with the tines of a fork. Divide the zucchini mixture equally among the pastry circles, add the tomatoes, leaving a ½-inch/1-cm border around the edge, and top each tart with a spoonful of goat cheese. Drizzle over 1 tablespoon of the remaining oil from the tomatoes and season to taste with salt and pepper.

Bake the tarts in the preheated oven for 10–15 minutes, or until golden brown and well risen. Serve warm.

SERVES 6
as part of a tapas meal

2½ oz/70 g sun-dried tomatoes in oil, drained and 2 tbsp oil reserved
1 zucchini, thinly sliced
1 garlic clove, crushed
9 oz/250 g puff pastry, thawed if frozen
5½ oz/150 g soft goat cheese
salt and pepper

figs with bleu cheese

SERVES 6
as part of a tapas meal

for the caramelized almonds
1/2 cup superfine sugar
4 oz/115 g blanched almonds
butter, for greasing

12 ripe figs
12 oz/350 g Spanish bleu
    cheese, such as Picós,
    crumbled
Spanish extra virgin olive oil,
    for drizzling

First make the caramelized almonds. Place the sugar in a pan over medium heat and stir until the sugar melts and turns golden brown and bubbles. Do not stir once the mixture begins to bubble. Remove the pan from the heat, then add the almonds one at a time and quickly turn with a fork until coated. If the caramel hardens, return the pan to the heat. Transfer each almond to a lightly greased baking sheet once it is coated. Let stand until cool and firm.

   For serving, slice the figs in half and arrange 4 halves on individual serving plates. Coarsely chop the almonds by hand. Place a mound of bleu cheese on each plate and sprinkle with chopped almonds. Drizzle the figs very lightly with the olive oil.

bleu cheese & bean salad

SERVES 4
as part of a tapas meal

scant 1 cup small dried great
   Northern beans, soaked for
   4 hours or overnight
1 bay leaf
4 tbsp Spanish olive oil
2 tbsp sherry vinegar
2 tsp clear honey
1 tsp Dijon mustard
salt and pepper
2 tbsp toasted slivered almonds
7 oz/200 g Cabrales or other
   bleu cheese, crumbled

Drain the beans and place in a large, heavy-bottom pan. Pour in enough water to cover, then add the bay leaf and bring to a boil. Boil for 1–1 1/2 hours, or until tender. Drain, then turn into a bowl and let cool slightly. Remove and discard the bay leaf.

Meanwhile, make the dressing. Whisk the olive oil, vinegar, honey, and mustard together in a bowl and season to taste with salt and pepper. Pour the dressing over the beans and toss lightly. Add the almonds and toss lightly again. Let cool to room temperature.

Spoon the beans into individual serving bowls and scatter over the cheese before serving.

bread

Bread and tapas is a culinary marriage made in heaven. Spaniards don't consider a meal complete without bread, and tapas are no exception. In Barcelona, for example, it's second nature to have a slice of Tomato Bread when stopping at a bar. Visit any tapas bar throughout the country and there will be a selection of salads on bread—creamy mayonnaise-based salads, such as tuna salad, potato salad, Russian salad (a mix of finely diced vegetables), or tender flakes of salt cod. In this chapter you will find plenty of ideas for quick and easy toast toppings as well as a selection of delicious dips and pâtés. There are also recipes for Spanish-style flatbreads and pizzas, not to mention Chorizo Bread Pockets—tiny balls of dough with a meaty filling.

catalan toasts

SERVES 8
as part of a tapas meal

2 garlic cloves
2 large tomatoes
pepper
8 slices day-old French bread
  or small rounds country
  bread or sourdough bread,
  about 3/4 inch/2 cm thick
choice of toppings such as
  slices of Serrano ham, slices
  of Manchego cheese, or
  pieces of roasted red bell
  pepper (optional)
3 tbsp Spanish extra virgin
  olive oil

Preheat the broiler to high. Halve the garlic cloves. Coarsely grate the tomatoes into a bowl, discarding the skins left in your hand, and season to taste with pepper.

Toast the bread slices under the broiler until lightly golden brown on both sides. While the bread slices are still warm, rub with the cut side of the garlic halves to flavor, then top with the grated tomatoes. If using, add a slice of ham or Manchego cheese or a piece of roasted red bell pepper. Drizzle each with a little of the oil and serve immediately.

chorizo bread pockets

SERVES 4
as part of a tapas meal

scant 1¹/₂ cups white bread
    flour, plus extra for dusting
1¹/₂ tsp active dry yeast
¹/₂ tsp salt
¹/₄ tsp superfine sugar
¹/₂ cup warm water
sunflower oil, for oiling
4 oz/115 g chorizo sausage,
    outer casing removed
aïoli (see page 50), for serving

To make the bread dough, put the flour, yeast, salt, and sugar in a large bowl and make a well in the center. Pour the water into the well and gradually mix in the flour from the side. Using your hands, mix together to form a soft dough that leaves the side of the bowl clean.

Turn the dough onto a lightly floured counter and knead for 10 minutes, or until smooth and elastic and no longer sticky. Shape the dough into a ball and put in a clean bowl. Cover with a clean, damp dish towel and leave in a warm place for 1 hour, or until the dough has risen and doubled in size.

Preheat the oven to 400°F/200°C. Oil a cookie sheet. Cut the chorizo sausage into 16 equal-size chunks. Turn out the risen dough onto a lightly floured counter and knead lightly for 2–3 minutes to knock out the air.

Divide the dough into 16 equal-size pieces. Shape each piece into a ball and roll out on a lightly floured counter to a 4¹/₂-inch/12-cm circle. Put a piece of chorizo on each circle and gather the dough at the top, enclosing the chorizo, then pinch the edges together well to seal. Put each dough pocket, pinched-side down, on the prepared cookie sheet.

Bake in the preheated oven for 20 minutes, or until pale golden brown. Turn the pockets over so that the pinched ends are facing up and arrange in a serving basket. Serve hot, as soon after baking as possible, because the pockets become dry on standing. Accompany with a bowl of aïoli for dipping, if using.

spicy fried bread
& chorizo

Cut the chorizo into ¹/₂-inch/1-cm thick slices and cut the bread, with its crusts still on, into ¹/₂-inch/1-cm cubes. Add enough olive oil to a large, heavy-bottom skillet so that it generously covers the base. Heat the oil, then add the garlic and cook for 30 seconds–1 minute, or until lightly browned.

Add the bread cubes to the pan and cook, stirring constantly, until golden brown and crisp. Add the chorizo slices and cook for 1–2 minutes, or until hot. Using a slotted spoon, remove the bread cubes and chorizo from the skillet and drain well on paper towels.

Turn the bread and chorizo into a warmed serving bowl, then add the chopped parsley and toss together. Garnish the dish with a sprinkling of paprika and serve warm. Accompany with wooden toothpicks so that a piece of sausage and a cube of bread can be speared together for eating.

SERVES 6–8
as part of a tapas meal

7 oz/200 g chorizo sausage, outer casing removed
4 thick slices 2-day-old country bread
Spanish olive oil, for pan-frying
3 garlic cloves, finely chopped
2 tbsp chopped fresh flat-leaf parsley
paprika, for garnish

chorizo & quail egg toasts

SERVES 6
as part of a tapas meal

12 slices French bread, sliced
 on the diagonal, about
 1/4 inch/5 mm thick
about 1 1/2 oz/40 g cured,
 ready-to-eat chorizo, cut into
 thin slices
olive oil
12 quail eggs
mild paprika
salt and pepper

Preheat the broiler to high. Arrange the slices of bread on a baking sheet and broil until golden brown on both sides.

Cut or fold the chorizo slices to fit on the toasts; set aside. Heat a thin layer of oil in a large skillet over medium heat until a cube of day-old bread sizzles—this takes about 40 seconds. Break the eggs into the skillet and cook, spooning the fat over the yolks, until the whites are set and the yolks are cooked to your liking.

Remove the cooked eggs from the skillet and drain on paper towels. Immediately transfer to the chorizo-topped toasts and dust with paprika. Sprinkle with salt and pepper to taste, and serve at once.

salt cod on garlic toasts

SERVES 6
as part of a tapas meal

7 oz/200 g dried salt cod
5 garlic cloves
1 cup olive oil
1 cup heavy cream
pepper
6 thick slices country bread

Soak the dried salt cod in cold water for 48 hours, changing the water 3 times a day. Drain well, then cut into chunks and place in a large, shallow skillet. Pour in enough cold water to cover and bring to a simmer. Poach for 8–10 minutes, or until tender. Drain well and let stand until cool enough to handle.

Finely chop 4 of the garlic cloves. Halve the remaining clove and reserve until needed.

Remove and discard the skin from the fish. Coarsely chop the flesh and place in a food processor or blender.

Pour the olive oil into a pan and add the chopped garlic. Bring to a simmer over low heat. Pour the cream into a separate pan and bring to a simmer over low heat. Remove both pans from the heat.

Process the fish briefly. With the motor still running, add a little of the garlic oil and process. With the motor still running, add a little cream and process. Continue in this way until all the garlic oil and cream have been incorporated. Scrape the mixture into a serving bowl and season to taste with pepper.

Toast the bread on both sides, then rub each slice with the cut sides of the reserved garlic. Pile the fish mixture onto the toasts and serve.

shrimp toasties

Halve 1 of the garlic cloves and reserve. Finely chop the remaining cloves. Heat 2 tablespoons of the olive oil in a large, heavy-bottom skillet. Add the chopped garlic and onion and cook over low heat, stirring occasionally, for 5 minutes, or until softened.

Stir in the beans and tomatoes and season to taste with salt and pepper. Cook gently for an additional 5 minutes.

Meanwhile, toast the bread on both sides, then rub each slice with the cut sides of the reserved garlic and drizzle with the remaining oil.

Stir the shrimp into the bean mixture and heat through gently for 2–3 minutes. Pile the bean and shrimp mixture onto the toasts and serve immediately, garnished with watercress.

SERVES 4
as part of a tapas meal

3 garlic cloves
4 tbsp Spanish olive oil
1 Spanish onion, halved and finely chopped
14 oz/400 g canned great Northern beans, drained and rinsed
4 tomatoes, diced
salt and pepper
4 thick slices country bread
10 oz/280 g cooked shelled shrimp
watercress, for garnish

roman dip with anchovy circles

SERVES 12
as part of a tapas meal

1 egg
scant 1 cup pitted black
    Spanish olives
1³/₄ oz/50 g canned anchovy
    fillets in olive oil, drained and
    oil reserved
2 garlic cloves, 1 crushed and
    1 peeled but kept whole
1 tbsp capers
¹/₂ tsp hot or sweet smoked
    Spanish paprika
1 tbsp Spanish brandy or sherry
4 tbsp Spanish extra virgin
    olive oil
pepper
1 small French bread

Put the egg in a pan, then cover with cold water and slowly bring to a boil. Reduce the heat and simmer gently for 10 minutes. Immediately drain the egg and rinse under cold running water to cool. Gently tap the egg to crack the shell and leave until cold.

When the egg is cold, crack the shell all over and remove it. Put the egg in a food processor and add the olives, 2 of the anchovy fillets, the crushed garlic, capers, paprika, and brandy and process to a coarse paste. With the motor running, very slowly add 1 tablespoon of the reserved oil from the anchovies and the extra virgin olive oil in a thin, steady stream. Season the dip to taste with pepper.

Turn the dip into a small serving bowl, then cover and chill in the refrigerator until ready to serve. To make the anchovy circles, put the remaining anchovy fillets, remaining reserved oil from the anchovies, and garlic clove in a mortar and, using a pestle, pound together to a paste. Turn the paste into a bowl, then cover and chill in the refrigerator until ready to serve.

When ready to serve, preheat the broiler to high. Cut the French bread into 1-inch/2.5-cm slices and toast under the broiler until golden brown on both sides. Spread the anchovy paste very thinly on the toasted bread circles and serve with the dip.

onion & olive circles

**SERVES 4–8
as part of a tapas meal**

2 tbsp Spanish olive oil
1 onion, thinly sliced
1 garlic clove, finely chopped
2 tsp chopped fresh thyme
salt and pepper
1 small French bread
1 tbsp tapenade or butter
8 canned anchovy fillets in oil,
   drained
12 green Spanish olives stuffed
   with almonds or onion, halved

Heat the olive oil in a heavy-bottom skillet. Add the onion and garlic and cook over low heat, stirring occasionally, for 15 minutes, or until golden brown and very soft. Stir in the thyme and season to taste with salt and pepper.

Meanwhile, cut off and discard the crusty ends of the bread, then cut the loaf into 8 slices. Toast on both sides, then spread one side with tapenade or butter.

Pile the onion mixture onto the slices of toast and top each slice with an anchovy fillet and the olives. Serve hot.

anchovy rolls

Preheat the oven to 425°F/220°C. Lightly grease a baking sheet. Place the anchovies in a small, shallow dish and pour over the milk. Let soak for 10–15 minutes. Drain, discarding the milk, and pat dry with paper towels.

Spread each bread slice with butter and then with mustard. Sprinkle with the grated cheese. Divide the anchovy among the bread slices and roll up.

Place on the baking sheet, seam-side down, and bake in the preheated oven for 6–7 minutes. Let cool slightly, then serve.

SERVES 4
as part of a tapas meal

butter, for greasing and
   spreading
8 salted anchovies
¼ cup milk
4 slices white bread, crusts
   removed
1 tbsp Dijon mustard
2 tbsp grated Manchego or
   Cheddar cheese

salads on bread

**each salad quantity SERVES 6
as part of a tapas meal**

for the potato salad
7 oz/200 g new potatoes,
  scrubbed and boiled
1/2 tbsp white wine vinegar
salt and pepper
3–4 tbsp mayonnaise
2 hard-cooked eggs, shelled
  and finely chopped
2 scallions, white and green
  parts finely chopped
1 large French bread

for the tuna salad
7 oz/200 g canned tuna in olive
  oil, drained
4 tbsp mayonnaise
2 hard-cooked eggs, shelled
  and finely chopped
1 tomato, roasted and peeled,
  seeded, and very finely
  chopped
2 tsp grated lemon rind,
  or to taste
cayenne pepper, to taste
salt and pepper
1 large French bread
12 anchovy fillets in oil,
  drained, for garnish

To make the potato salad, peel the potatoes as soon as they are cool enough to handle, then cut into 1/4-inch/5-mm dice. Toss with the vinegar and season to taste with salt and pepper. Let cool completely. Stir in the mayonnaise, then fold in the eggs and scallions. Taste and adjust the seasoning. Cut the bread on a slight diagonal into 12 slices, 1/4 inch/5 mm thick. Mound the salad onto the bread.

To make the tuna salad, flake the tuna into a bowl. Stir in the mayonnaise, then fold in the eggs, tomato, lemon rind, and cayenne. Taste and adjust the seasoning. Cut the bread on a slight diagonal into 12 slices, 1/4 inch/5 mm thick. Mound the salad on the bread, then top with anchovy fillets.

flatbread with vegetables & clams

SERVES 4–6
as part of a tapas meal

2 tbsp Spanish extra virgin
   olive oil
4 large garlic cloves, crushed
2 large onions, thinly sliced
10 pimientos del piquillo,
   drained, patted dry, and
   thinly sliced
9 oz/250 g shelled baby clams
   in brine (weight in jar),
   drained and rinsed
salt and pepper

for the dough
$2^2/3$ cups white bread flour,
   plus extra for dusting
1 envelope active dry yeast
1 tsp salt
$1/2$ tsp sugar
1 tbsp Spanish olive oil, plus
   extra for oiling
1 tbsp dry white wine
1 cup warm water

To make the dough, stir the flour, yeast, salt, and sugar together in a bowl, making a well in the center. Add the olive oil and wine to the water, then pour $1/4$ cup of the liquid into the well. Gradually mix in the flour from the sides, adding the remaining liquid if necessary, until a soft dough forms.

Turn out the dough onto a lightly floured counter and knead until smooth. Shape the dough into a ball. Wash the bowl and rub the inside with olive oil. Return the dough to the bowl and roll it around until lightly coated in oil. Cover the bowl tightly with plastic wrap and let stand in a warm place until the dough doubles in size.

Heat the olive oil in a large, heavy-bottom skillet over medium heat. Reduce the heat and add the garlic and onions and cook slowly, stirring frequently, for 25 minutes, or until the onions are golden brown but not burned.

Preheat the oven to 450°F/230°C. Transfer the onions to a bowl and let cool. Add the pimiento del piquillo strips and clams to the bowl and stir together. Reserve.

Punch the dough and knead quickly on a lightly floured counter. Cover it with the upturned bowl and let stand for 10 minutes, which will make it easier to roll out.

Heavily flour a $12^3/4 \times 12^3/4$-inch/32 × 32-cm shallow baking sheet. Roll out the dough to make a $13^1/2$-inch/34-cm square and transfer it to the baking sheet, rolling the edges to form a thin rim. Prick the base all over with a fork.

Spread the topping evenly over the dough and season to taste with salt and pepper. Bake in the preheated oven for 25 minutes, or until the rim is golden brown and the onion tips are slightly tinged. Transfer to a wire rack to cool completely. Cut into 12–16 slices.

artichoke & pimiento flatbread

To make the bread dough, put the flour, yeast, salt, and sugar in a large bowl and make a well in the center. Mix the water and oil together in a pitcher and pour into the well, then gradually mix in the flour from the side. Using your hands, mix together to form a soft dough that leaves the side of the bowl clean.

Turn out the dough onto a lightly floured counter and knead for 10 minutes, or until smooth and elastic and no longer sticky. Shape the dough into a ball and put in a clean bowl. Cover with a clean, damp dish towel and leave in a warm place for 1 hour, or until the dough has risen and doubled in size.

Meanwhile, heat 3 tablespoons of the oil in a large skillet, then add the onions and cook over medium heat, stirring occasionally, for 10 minutes, or until golden brown. Add the garlic and cook, stirring, for 30 seconds, or until softened. Let cool. When cool, stir in the artichoke hearts and pimientos del piquillo, then season to taste with salt and pepper.

Preheat the oven to 400°F/200°C. Oil a large cookie sheet. Turn out the risen dough onto a lightly floured counter and knead lightly for 2–3 minutes to knock out the air. Roll out the dough to a 12-inch/30-cm square and transfer to the prepared cookie sheet.

Brush the remaining oil over the dough and spread the artichoke and pimiento mixture on top. Sprinkle over the olives, if using. Bake in the preheated oven for 20–25 minutes, or until golden brown and crisp. Cut into 12 slices and serve hot or warm.

SERVES 4–6
as part of a tapas meal

4 tbsp Spanish olive oil, plus
  extra for oiling
2 large onions, thinly sliced
2 garlic cloves, finely chopped
14 oz/400 g canned artichoke
  hearts, drained and quartered
11¼ oz/320 g bottled or canned
  pimientos del piquillo,
  drained and thinly sliced
salt and pepper
scant ¼ cup pitted black
  Spanish olives (optional)

for the bread dough
heaping 2¾ cups white bread
  flour, plus extra for dusting
1½ tsp active dry yeast
1 tsp salt
½ tsp superfine sugar
¾ cup warm water
3 tbsp Spanish olive oil

sun-dried tomato
toasts with goat cheese

SERVES 6
as part of a tapas meal

2 tbsp Spanish extra virgin
   olive oil, plus extra for oiling
8 oz/225 g soft goat cheese
2 tsp freshly squeezed lemon
   juice
2 garlic cloves, crushed
1 tsp hot or sweet smoked
   Spanish paprika
heaping 1/8 cup pitted green
   Spanish olives, finely chopped
1 tbsp chopped fresh flat-leaf
   parsley

for the sun-dried tomato toasts
1 3/4 oz/50 g sun-dried tomatoes
   in oil, drained and 3 tbsp oil
   reserved
1 garlic clove, crushed
1 long French bread

Preheat the oven to 400°F/200°C. Generously oil a cookie sheet. To make the toasts, very finely chop the tomatoes and put in a bowl. Add the reserved oil from the tomatoes and the garlic and mix together well.

Slice the bread into 1/2-inch/1-cm thick slices and spread with the tomato mixture. Put on the prepared cookie sheet and bake in the preheated oven for 10 minutes, or until golden brown and crisp. Let cool on a cooling rack.

To make the dip, put the goat cheese in a food processor. With the motor running, add 1 tablespoon of the oil, drop by drop. Using a spatula, scrape down the side of the bowl. With the motor running again, very slowly add the remaining oil and the lemon juice in a thin, steady stream. Add the garlic and paprika and process until well mixed.

Stir the olives and parsley into the dip. Turn the dip into a small serving bowl, then cover and chill in the refrigerator for at least 1 hour before serving.

Serve the dip accompanied by the toasts.

fresh mint & bean pâté

SERVES 12
as part of a tapas meal

1 lb 12 oz/800 g fresh fava
   beans in their pods, shelled
   to give about 12 oz/350 g
8 oz/225 g soft goat cheese
1 garlic clove, crushed
2 scallions, finely chopped
1 tbsp Spanish extra virgin olive
   oil, plus extra for serving
grated rind and 2 tbsp lemon
   juice
about 60 large fresh mint
   leaves, about $^1/_2$ oz/15 g
   in total
salt and pepper
12 slices French bread

Cook the fava beans in a pan of boiling water for 8–10 minutes, or until tender. Drain well and let cool. When the beans are cool enough to handle, slip off their skins and put the beans in a food processor. This is a laborious task, but worth doing if you have the time. This quantity will take about 15 minutes to skin.

Add the goat cheese, garlic, scallions, oil, lemon rind and juice, and mint leaves to the fava beans and process until well mixed. Season the pâté to taste with salt and pepper. Turn into a bowl, cover, then chill in the refrigerator for at least 1 hour before serving.

To serve, preheat the broiler to high. Toast the bread slices under the broiler until golden brown on both sides. Drizzle a little oil over the toasted bread slices, then spread the pâté on top and serve immediately.

eggplant & bell pepper dip

Preheat the oven to 375°F/190°C. Prick the skins of the eggplants and bell peppers all over with a fork and brush with 1 tablespoon of the olive oil. Place on a baking sheet and bake in the preheated oven for 45 minutes, or until the skins are beginning to turn black, the flesh of the eggplant is very soft, and the bell peppers are deflated.

Place the cooked vegetables in a bowl and cover tightly with a clean, damp dish towel. Alternatively, place the vegetables in a plastic bag and let stand for about 15 minutes, or until cool enough to handle.

When the vegetables have cooled, cut the eggplants in half lengthwise, carefully scoop out the flesh, and discard the skin. Cut the eggplant flesh into large chunks. Remove and discard the stem, core, and seeds from the bell peppers and cut the flesh into large pieces.

Heat the remaining olive oil in a skillet. Add the eggplant and bell pepper and cook for 5 minutes. Add the garlic and cook for 30 seconds.

Turn the contents of the skillet onto paper towels to drain, then transfer to a food processor. Add the lemon rind and juice, the chopped cilantro, the paprika, and salt and pepper to taste, then process until a speckled purée is formed.

Transfer the eggplant and bell pepper dip to a serving bowl. Serve warm, at room temperature, or let cool for 30 minutes, then let chill in the refrigerator for at least 1 hour and serve cold. Garnish with cilantro sprigs and accompany with thick slices of bread or toast for dipping.

SERVES 6–8
as part of a tapas meal

2 large eggplants
2 red bell peppers
4 tbsp Spanish olive oil
2 garlic cloves, coarsely
    chopped
grated rind and juice of
    1/2 lemon
1 tbsp chopped cilantro, plus
    extra sprigs for garnish
1/2–1 tsp paprika
salt and pepper
bread or toast, for serving

wild mushroom
& aïoli toasts

SERVES 6
as part of a tapas meal

5 tbsp Spanish olive oil
2 large garlic cloves, finely
  chopped
1 lb/450 g wild, exotic, or
  cultivated mushrooms, sliced
2 tbsp dry Spanish sherry
4 tbsp chopped fresh
  flat-leaf parsley
salt and pepper
12 slices long, thick crusty
  bread
8 tbsp aïoli (see page 50)

Heat the oil in a large skillet, then add the garlic and cook over medium heat, stirring, for 30 seconds, or until softened. Increase the heat to high, then add the mushrooms and cook, stirring constantly, until the mushrooms are coated in the oil and all the oil has been absorbed.

Reduce the heat to low and cook for 2–3 minutes, or until all the juices have been released from the mushrooms. Add the sherry, increase the heat to high again and cook, stirring frequently, for 3–4 minutes until the liquid has evaporated. Stir in the parsley and season to taste with salt and pepper.

Meanwhile, preheat the broiler to high. Toast the bread slices under the broiler until lightly golden brown on both sides.

Spread the aïoli on top of each toast and top with the cooked mushrooms. Carefully transfer the toasts to a broiler rack and cook under the broiler until the aïoli starts to bubble. Serve hot.

roasted red bell peppers on garlic toasts

SERVES 4
as part of a tapas meal

4 thin slices white country
    bread
5 tbsp Spanish olive oil
2 large garlic cloves, crushed
3 large red bell peppers
pepper
chopped fresh flat-leaf parsley,
    for garnish

Preheat the oven to 450°F/230°C. To make the garlic toasts, halve each bread slice. Put 3 tablespoons of the oil in a bowl and stir in the garlic. Brush each side of the bread slice halves with the oil mixture and transfer to a cookie sheet. Bake in the preheated oven for 10–15 minutes, or until crisp and golden brown. Let cool on paper towels.

Reduce the oven temperature to 400°F/200°C. Brush the red bell peppers with the remaining oil and put in a roasting pan. Roast in the oven for 30 minutes, then turn over and roast for an additional 10 minutes, or until the skins have blistered and blackened.

Using a slotted spoon, transfer the roasted peppers to a plastic bag and leave for 15 minutes, or until cool enough to handle.

Using a sharp knife or your fingers, carefully peel away the skin from the peppers. Halve the bell peppers and remove the stems, cores, and seeds, then cut each bell pepper into neat, thin strips.

For serving, arrange the bell pepper strips on top of the garlic toasts. Season to taste with pepper and sprinkle with chopped parsley for garnish.

tomato bread

If the bread is soft, toast it under a preheated broiler until lightly golden on both sides. Rub each slice of bread with half a fresh juicy tomato. If using, sprinkle over the chopped garlic and drizzle the olive oil over the top.

SERVES 4
as part of a tapas meal

4 slices French bread
2 ripe tomatoes, halved
1 garlic clove, finely chopped
 (optional)
2 tbsp Spanish olive oil
 (optional)

asparagus rolls

SERVES 8
as part of a tapas meal

1/2 cup butter, softened, plus
   extra for greasing
8 asparagus spears, trimmed
8 slices white bread, crusts
   removed
1 tbsp chopped fresh parsley
finely grated rind of 1 orange
salt and pepper

Preheat the oven to 375°F/190°C and lightly grease a baking sheet. If woody, peel the asparagus stems, then tie the spears loosely together with clean kitchen string. Blanch in a tall pan of boiling water for 3–5 minutes. Drain and refresh under cold running water. Drain again and pat dry with paper towels.

Lightly flatten the slices of bread with a rolling pin. Mix half of the butter, the parsley, and orange rind together in a bowl and season to taste with salt and pepper. Spread the flavored butter over the bread slices.

Place an asparagus spear near one side of a bread slice and roll up. Repeat with the remaining asparagus spears and bread. Place the asparagus rolls, seam-side down, on the baking sheet.

Melt the remaining butter in a small pan, then brush it over the asparagus rolls. Bake in the preheated oven for 15 minutes, or until crisp and golden brown. Let cool slightly, then serve warm.

spinach & tomato pizzas

SERVES 16
as part of a tapas meal

2 tbsp Spanish olive oil, plus
   extra for brushing and
   drizzling
1 onion, finely chopped
1 garlic clove, finely chopped
14 oz/400 g canned chopped
   tomatoes
4¹/₂ oz/125 g fresh baby spinach
salt and pepper
2 tbsp pine nuts

for the bread dough
scant ¹/₂ cup warm water
¹/₂ tsp active dry yeast
pinch of sugar
1¹/₃ cups white bread flour,
   plus extra for dusting
¹/₂ tsp salt

To make the bread dough, measure the water into a small bowl. Sprinkle in the dried yeast and sugar and let stand in a warm place for 10–15 minutes, or until frothy.

Meanwhile, sift the flour and salt into a large bowl. Make a well in the center and pour in the yeast liquid, then mix together with a spoon. Using your hands, work the mixture until it leaves the sides of the bowl clean.

Turn the dough out onto a lightly floured counter and knead for 10 minutes, or until smooth and elastic and no longer sticky. Shape into a ball and put it in a clean bowl. Cover with a clean, damp kitchen towel and let stand in a warm place for 1 hour, or until it has risen and doubled in size.

To make the topping, heat the olive oil in a large, heavy-bottom skillet. Add the onion and cook for 5 minutes, or until softened but not browned. Add the garlic and cook for an additional 30 seconds. Stir in the tomatoes and cook for 5 minutes, letting it bubble and stirring occasionally, until reduced to a thick mixture. Add the spinach leaves and cook, stirring, until they have wilted slightly. Season to taste with salt and pepper.

While the dough is rising, preheat the oven to 400°F/200°C. Brush several baking sheets with olive oil. Turn the dough out onto a lightly floured counter and knead well for 2–3 minutes to knock out the air bubbles.

Roll out the dough very, very thinly and, using a 2¹/₂-inch/6-cm plain, round cutter, cut out 32 circles. Place on the prepared baking sheets.

Spread each base with the spinach mixture to cover, then sprinkle the pine nuts over the top. Drizzle a little olive oil over each pizza. Bake in the preheated oven for 10–15 minutes, or until the edges of the dough are golden brown. Serve the spinach and tomato pizzas hot.

aïoli
  baby potatoes with aïoli 50
  chorizo bread pockets 184
  crispy chicken & ham croquettes 82
  deep-fried artichoke hearts 26
  rosemary skewers with monkfish & bacon 104
  Serrano ham croquettes 73
  stuffed cherry tomatoes 32
  wild mushroom & aïoli toasts 212
almonds 11
  bleu cheese & bean salad 178
  calves' liver in almond saffron sauce 61
  figs with bleu cheese 176
  salted almonds 14
  sardines with romesco sauce 100
  spinach & mushroom tortilla 146
  tiny meatballs in almond sauce 64
anchovies
  anchovy rolls 199
  empanadillas with cheese & olives 172
  onion & olive circles 196
  Roman dip with anchovy circles 194
  salads on bread 200
  stuffed cherry tomatoes 32
  stuffed eggs with anchovies & cheese 152
artichokes
  artichoke & pimiento flatbread 205
  deep-fried artichoke hearts 26
asparagus
  asparagus & fried eggs 157
  asparagus rolls 218
  asparagus scrambled eggs 158
  baby leek & asparagus salad 38

baby leek & asparagus salad 38
baby potatoes with aïoli 50
bacon: rosemary skewers with monkfish & bacon 104
baked tomato nests 164
basil: chicken wings with tomato dressing 91
Basque scrambled eggs 160
batter-fried fish sticks 109
beef
  beef skewers with orange & garlic 58
  porterhouse steak with garlic & sherry 56
  tiny meatballs in almond sauce 64
bell peppers
  Basque scrambled eggs 160
  beef skewers with orange & garlic 58
  bell peppers with fiery cheese 170
  Catalan toasts 182
  chorizo & mushroom kabobs 80
  eggplant & bell pepper dip 211
  flamenco eggs 163
  fresh salmon with red bell pepper sauce 103
  oven-baked tortilla 142
  roasted bell pepper salad 44
  roasted red bell peppers on garlic toasts 214
  sardines with romesco sauce 100
  simmered summer vegetables 34
  summer salad in a tomato dressing 43
  sweet peppers stuffed with crab salad 127
  tossed shrimp with bell peppers 118
  tuna-stuffed bell pepper strips 110
  see also pimientos
bleu cheese & bean salad 178

breads
  anchovy rolls 199
  artichoke & pimiento flatbread 205
  asparagus rolls 218
  asparagus scrambled eggs 158
  Basque scrambled eggs 160
  Catalan toasts 182
  chorizo & quail egg toasts 188
  chorizo bread pockets 184
  flatbread with vegetables & clams 202
  fresh mint & bean pâté 208
  onion & olive circles 196
  roasted red bell peppers on garlic toasts 214
  Roman dip with anchovy circles 194
  salads on bread 200
  salt cod on garlic toasts 190
  shrimp toasties 193
  spicy fried bread & chorizo 187
  spinach & tomato pizzas 220
  sun-dried tomato toasts with goat cheese 206
  tomato bread 217
  wild mushroom & aïoli toasts 212

calamari with shrimp & fava beans 116
calves' liver in almond saffron sauce 61
capers
  baby leek & asparagus salad 38
  empanadillas with ham & goat cheese 74
  mussels in vinaigrette dressing 130
  roasted bell pepper salad 44
  Roman dip with anchovy circles 194
  stuffed cherry tomatoes 32
  summer salad in a tomato dressing 43
Catalan toasts 182
charcuterie 11
cheese 11
  anchovy rolls 199
  baked tomato nests 164
  bell peppers with fiery cheese 170
  bleu cheese & bean salad 178
  Catalan toasts 182
  cheese puffs with fiery tomato salsa 166
  crab tartlets 124
  eggs & cheese 154
  empanadillas with cheese & olives 172
  figs with bleu cheese 176
  fried Manchego cheese 169
  oven-baked tortilla 142
  pickled stuffed sweet peppers 31
  spinach & mushroom tortilla 146
  stuffed eggs with anchovies & cheese 152
  see also goat cheese; soft cheese
chicken
  chicken livers in sherry sauce 92
  chicken rolls with olives 86
  chicken salad with raisins & pine nuts 94
  chicken wings with tomato dressing 91
  crispy chicken & ham croquettes 82
  Moroccan chicken kabobs 88
  sautéed chicken with crispy garlic slices 85
chickpeas & chorizo 79
chiles
  cheese puffs with fiery tomato salsa 166
  deep-fried green chiles 20
  eggs & cheese 154
  mixed seafood kabobs with chili & lime glaze 106
  mussels in vinaigrette dressing 130

orange & fennel salad 46
patatas bravas 49
sardines with romesco sauce 100
sizzling chile shrimp 121
spicy cracked marinated olives 16
chives
  eggs & cheese 154
  mussels with garlic butter 133
  oven-baked tortilla 142
chorizo
  Basque scrambled eggs 160
  chickpeas & chorizo 79
  chorizo & fava bean tortilla 145
  chorizo & mushroom kabobs 80
  chorizo & quail egg toasts 188
  chorizo bread pockets 184
  chorizo in red wine 76
  spicy fried bread & chorizo 187
cilantro
  eggplant & bell pepper dip 211
  zucchini salad with cilantro dressing 40
cinnamon
  Moroccan chicken kabobs 88
  olives with orange & lemon 19
clams
  clams in tomato & garlic sauce 136
  flatbread with vegetables & clams 202
cod, salt
  salt cod fritters with spinach 98
  salt cod on garlic toasts 190
coriander
  lamb skewers with lemon 62
  Moroccan chicken kabobs 88
  Spanish meatballs with cracked olives 67
  spicy cracked marinated olives 16
corn: flamenco eggs 163
crabmeat
  crab tartlets 124
  stuffed cherry tomatoes 32
  sweet peppers stuffed with crab salad 127
crispy chicken & ham croquettes 82
cumin
  chicken wings with tomato dressing 91
  lamb skewers with lemon 62
  Moroccan chicken kabobs 88
  olives with orange & lemon 19
  Spanish meatballs with cracked olives 67
  zucchini salad with cilantro dressing 40

deep-fried artichoke hearts 26
deep-fried green chiles 20
deviled eggs 151
dill: pickled stuffed sweet peppers 31

eggplants
  eggplant & bell pepper dip 211
  eggplant tortilla wedges 148
  marinated eggplants 28
  simmered summer vegetables 34
eggs
  asparagus & fried eggs 157
  asparagus scrambled eggs 158
  baby leek & asparagus salad 38
  baked tomato nests 164
  Basque scrambled eggs 160
  cheese puffs with fiery tomato salsa 166
  chorizo & fava bean tortilla 145
  chorizo & quail egg toasts 188

clams in tomato & garlic sauce 136
deviled eggs 151
eggplant tortilla wedges 148
eggs & cheese 154
flamenco eggs 163
oven-baked tortilla 142
salads on bread 200
Spanish tortilla 140
spinach & mushroom tortilla 146
stuffed cherry tomatoes 32
stuffed eggs with anchovies & cheese 152
summer salad in tomato dressing 43
empanadillas
empanadillas with cheese & olives 172
empanadillas with ham & goat cheese 74
empanadillas with tuna & olives 112

fava beans
calamari with shrimp & fava beans 116
chorizo & fava bean tortilla 145
fava beans with ham 37
fresh mint & bean pâté 208
fennel
orange & fennel salad 46
spicy cracked marinated olives 16
fennel seeds: olives with orange & lemon 19
figs with bleu cheese 176
flamenco eggs 163
flatbread
artichoke & pimiento flatbread 205
flatbread with vegetables & clams 202
fresh mint & bean pâté 208
fresh salmon with red bell pepper sauce 103
fried Manchego cheese 169

garlic 11
artichoke & pimiento flatbread 205
baby potatoes with aïoli 50
beef skewers with orange & garlic 58
calamari with shrimp & fava beans 116
calves' liver in almond saffron sauce 61
Catalan toasts 182
chicken livers in sherry sauce 92
chicken wings with tomato dressing 91
clams in tomato & garlic sauce 136
deep-fried artichoke hearts 26
eggplant & bell pepper dip 211
flamenco eggs 163
flatbread with vegetables & clams 202
lamb skewers with lemon 62
marinated eggplants 28
miniature pork brochettes 70
Moroccan chicken kabobs 88
mussels with garlic butter 133
patatas bravas 49
porterhouse steak with garlic & sherry 56
potato wedges with shallots & rosemary 52
roasted bell pepper salad 44
roasted red bell peppers on garlic toasts 214
Roman dip with anchovy circles 194
saffron shrimp with lemon mayonnaise 122
salt cod on garlic toasts 190
sardines with romesco sauce 100
sautéed chicken with crispy garlic slices 85
sautéed garlic mushrooms 22
scallops with Serrano ham 128
seared squid & golden potatoes 115

shrimp toasties 193
simmered summer vegetables 34
sizzling chile shrimp 121
Spanish meatballs with cracked olives 67
spareribs coated in paprika sauce 68
spicy cracked marinated olives 16
spicy fried bread & chorizo 187
sun-dried tomato toasts with goat cheese 206
tiny meatballs in almond sauce 64
tossed shrimp with bell peppers 118
wild mushroom & aïoli toasts 212
zucchini salad with cilantro dressing 40
gherkins: summer salad in tomato dressing 43
ginger: mixed seafood kabobs with chili & lime glaze 106
goat cheese
empanadillas with ham & goat cheese 74
fresh mint & bean pâté 208
pickled stuffed sweet peppers 31
sun-dried tomato & goat cheese tarts 175
sun-dried tomato toasts with goat cheese 206
Great Northern beans
bleu cheese & bean salad 178
shrimp toasties 193
green beans: summer salad in a tomato dressing 43

hake
batter-fried fish sticks 109
mixed seafood kabobs with chili & lime glaze 106
ham 11
Catalan toasts 182
crispy chicken & ham croquettes 82
empanadillas with ham & goat cheese 74
fava beans with ham 37
scallops with Serrano ham 128
Serrano ham croquettes 73
honey
bell peppers with fiery cheese 170
bleu cheese & bean salad 178

lamb
lamb skewers with lemon 62
Spanish meatballs with cracked olives 67
tiny meatballs in almond sauce 64
leeks: baby leek & asparagus salad 38
legumes 11
lemons
chicken salad with raisins & pine nuts 94
deep-fried artichoke hearts 26
fresh mint & bean pâté 208
lamb skewers with lemon 62
marinated eggplants 28
miniature pork brochettes 70
Moroccan chicken kabobs 88
olives with orange & lemon 19
rosemary skewers with monkfish & bacon 104
saffron shrimp with lemon mayonnaise 122
scallops with Serrano ham 128
spicy cracked marinated olives 16
sun-dried tomato toasts with goat cheese 206
sweet peppers stuffed with crab salad 127
tossed shrimp with bell peppers 118
zucchini fritters with dipping sauce 25
limes: mixed seafood kabobs with chili & lime glaze 106
liver
calves' liver in almond saffron sauce 61

chicken livers in sherry sauce 92

marinated eggplants 28
marjoram
roasted bell pepper salad 44
sardines with romesco sauce 100
miniature pork brochettes 70
mint
fresh mint & bean pâté 208
olives with orange & lemon 19
mixed seafood kabobs with chili & lime glaze 106
monkfish
batter-fried fish sticks 109
mixed seafood kabobs with chili & lime glaze 106
rosemary skewers with monkfish & bacon 104
Moroccan chicken kabobs 88
mushrooms
chorizo & mushroom kabobs 80
sautéed garlic mushrooms 22
spinach & mushroom tortilla 146
wild mushroom & aïoli toasts 212
mussels
mussels in vinaigrette dressing 130
mussels with garlic butter 133

olive oil 11
olives
artichoke & pimiento flatbread 205
chicken rolls with olives 86
deviled eggs 151
empanadillas with cheese & olives 172
empanadillas with tuna & olives 112
olives with orange & lemon 19
onion & olive circles 196
orange & fennel salad 46
roasted bell pepper salad 44
Roman dip with anchovy circles 194
salads on bread 200
Spanish meatballs with cracked olives 67
spicy cracked marinated olives 16
stuffed cherry tomatoes 32
stuffed eggs with anchovies & cheese 152
summer salad in a tomato dressing 43
sun-dried tomato toasts with goat cheese 206
onion & olive circles 196
oranges
asparagus rolls 218
beef skewers with orange & garlic 58
olives with orange & lemon 19
orange & fennel salad 46
oregano
Moroccan chicken kabobs 88
spareribs coated in paprika sauce 68
oven-baked tortilla 142
oysters with sherry vinegar 134

paprika 11
cheese puffs with fiery tomato salsa 166
chorizo & quail egg toasts 188
deep-fried artichoke hearts 26
eggplant & bell pepper dip 211
empanadillas with ham & goat cheese 74
Moroccan chicken kabobs 88
patatas bravas 49
Roman dip with anchovy circles 194
salt cod fritters with spinach 98
sardines with romesco sauce 100

sautéed chicken with crispy garlic slices 85
Serrano ham croquettes 73
Spanish meatballs with cracked olives 67
spareribs coated in paprika sauce 68
summer salad in a tomato dressing 43
sun-dried tomato toasts with goat cheese 206
zucchini fritters with dipping sauce 25
parsley
    asparagus rolls 218
    baby potatoes with aïoli 50
    calamari with shrimp & fava beans 116
    chicken livers in sherry sauce 92
    chicken rolls with olives 86
    chicken salad with raisins & pine nuts 94
    clams in tomato & garlic sauce 136
    crab tartlets 124
    crispy chicken & ham croquettes 82
    fava beans with ham 37
    flamenco eggs 163
    marinated eggplants 28
    miniature pork brochettes 70
    mussels in vinaigrette dressing 130
    mussels with garlic butter 133
    olives with orange & lemon 19
    orange & fennel salad 46
    salt cod fritters with spinach 98
    sardines with romesco sauce 100
    sautéed garlic mushrooms 22
    scallops with Serrano ham 128
    seared squid & golden potatoes 115
    spicy fried bread & chorizo 187
    spinach & mushroom tortilla 146
    stuffed cherry tomatoes 32
    tiny meatballs in almond sauce 64
    tuna-stuffed bell pepper strips 110
    wild mushroom & aïoli toasts 212
    zucchini fritters with dipping sauce 25
    zucchini salad with cilantro dressing 40
pastry
    crab tartlets 124
    empanadillas with cheese & olives 172
    empanadillas with ham & goat cheese 74
    empanadillas with tuna & olives 112
    sun-dried tomato & goat cheese tarts 175
pickled stuffed sweet peppers 31
pimientos 11
    artichoke & pimiento flatbread 205
    chickpeas & chorizo 79
    deviled eggs 151
    flatbread with vegetables & clams 202
    pickled stuffed sweet peppers 31
    sweet peppers stuffed with crab salad 127
pine nuts
    chicken salad with raisins & pine nuts 94
    empanadillas with tuna & olives 112
    spinach & tomato pizzas 220
    zucchini fritters with dipping sauce 25
    zucchini salad with cilantro dressing 40
pork
    miniature pork brochettes 70
    Spanish meatballs with cracked olives 67
    spareribs coated in paprika sauce 68
    tiny meatballs in almond sauce 64
porterhouse steak with garlic & sherry 56
potatoes
    baby potatoes with aïoli 50
    oven-baked tortilla 142

patatas bravas 49
potato wedges with shallots & rosemary 52
salads on bread 200
seared squid & golden potatoes 115
Spanish tortilla 140

raisins: chicken salad with raisins & pine nuts 94
ras-el-hanout: miniature pork brochettes 70
roasted bell pepper salad 44
roasted red bell peppers on garlic toasts 214
Roman dip with anchovy circles 194
rosemary
    potato wedges with shallots & rosemary 52
    rosemary skewers with monkfish & bacon 104

saffron 11
    calves' liver in almond saffron sauce 61
    saffron shrimp with lemon mayonnaise 122
salads on bread 200
salmon
    fresh salmon with red bell pepper sauce 103
    mixed seafood kabobs with chili & lime glaze 106
salt cod
    salt cod fritters with spinach 98
    salt cod on garlic toasts 190
salted almonds 14
sardines with romesco sauce 100
sautéed chicken with crispy garlic slices 85
sautéed garlic mushrooms 22
scallops with Serrano ham 128
seared squid & golden potatoes 115
Serrano ham croquettes 73
shallots
    mussels in vinaigrette dressing 130
    oysters with sherry vinegar 134
    potato wedges with shallots & rosemary 52
    sardines with romesco sauce 100
    spinach & mushroom tortilla 146
sherry, sherry vinegar
    baby leek & asparagus salad 38
    bell peppers with fiery cheese 170
    bleu cheese & bean salad 178
    calves' liver in almond saffron sauce 61
    chicken livers in sherry sauce 92
    chickpeas & chorizo 79
    oysters with sherry vinegar 134
    patatas bravas 49
    porterhouse steak with garlic & sherry 56
    roasted bell pepper salad 44
    Roman dip with anchovy circles 194
    Spanish meatballs with cracked olives 67
    spareribs coated in paprika sauce 68
    summer salad in a tomato dressing 43
    tossed shrimp with bell peppers 118
    wild mushroom & aïoli toasts 212
shrimp
    calamari with shrimp & fava beans 116
    mixed seafood kabobs with chili & lime glaze 106
    saffron shrimp with lemon mayonnaise 122
    shrimp toasties 193
    sizzling chile shrimp 121
    tossed shrimp with bell peppers 118
simmered summer vegetables 34
sizzling chile shrimp 121
soft cheese
    sweet peppers stuffed with crab salad 127
    tuna-stuffed bell pepper strips 110

Spanish meatballs with cracked olives 67
Spanish tortilla 140
spareribs coated in paprika sauce 68
spicy cracked marinated olives 16
spicy fried bread & chorizo 187
spinach
    salt cod fritters with spinach 98
    spinach & mushroom tortilla 146
    spinach & tomato pizzas 220
squid
    calamari with shrimp & fava beans 116
    seared squid & golden potatoes 115
stuffed cherry tomatoes 32
stuffed eggs with anchovies & cheese 152
summer salad in a tomato dressing 43
sun-dried tomato & goat cheese tarts 175
sun-dried tomato toasts with goat cheese 206
sweet peppers stuffed with crab salad 127

tapas culture 8
thyme
    lamb skewers with lemon 62
    marinated eggplants 28
    onion & olive circles 196
    spicy cracked marinated olives 16
tiny meatballs in almond sauce 64
tomatoes
    baked tomato nests 164
    Basque scrambled eggs 160
    beef skewers with orange & garlic 58
    Catalan toasts 182
    cheese puffs with fiery tomato salsa 166
    chicken wings with tomato dressing 91
    clams in tomato & garlic sauce 136
    empanadillas with cheese & olives 172
    flamenco eggs 163
    patatas bravas 49
    salads on bread 200
    sardines with romesco sauce 100
    shrimp toasties 193
    simmered summer vegetables 34
    Spanish meatballs with cracked olives 67
    spinach & tomato pizzas 220
    stuffed cherry tomatoes 32
    summer salad in a tomato dressing 43
    sun-dried tomato & goat cheese tarts 175
    sun-dried tomato toasts with goat cheese 206
    tomato bread 217
tortilla
    chorizo & fava bean tortilla 145
    eggplant tortilla wedges 148
    oven-baked tortilla 142
    Spanish tortilla 140
    spinach & mushroom tortilla 146
tossed shrimp with bell peppers 118
tuna
    empanadillas with tuna & olives 112
    salads on bread 200
    tuna-stuffed bell pepper strips 110

wild mushroom & aïoli toasts 212

zucchini
    simmered summer vegetables 34
    sun-dried tomato & goat cheese tarts 175
    zucchini fritters with dipping sauce 25
    zucchini salad with cilantro dressing 40